THE VALSETZ STAR
— 2000 —

Dorothy Anne Hobson
and Ron Fowler

A nonfiction array of 1937–41, historical narratives from an
isolated lumber town, and whimsical writings from the talented
stubby pencil of a nine-year old editor

ALSO AVAILABLE BY RON FOWLER:

Self-Publishing the Write Way

ISBN 0-9654479-2-8 • $14⁹⁵ • 176 illustrated pages

This self-help book chronicles my experiences, often humorous, in writing, self-publishing, marketing, selling and distributing two successful (one was a flop) books during the past four years. Copies of The Valsetz Star or Self-Publishing the Write Way are available at your favorite bookseller or direct from the author, $14.95 plus $2.00 shipping and handling (Washington residents add $1.26 sales tax)

Ron Fowler
44 Leschi Drive
Steilacoom, WA 98388
Phone: (253) 584-0712

First edition

Library of Congress control Number 00-133104
ISBN 0-9654479-3-6

Proudly printed by Gorham Printing,
Rochester, WA 98579
Phone: 1-800-837-0970

Cover, Layout, and text arrangement by Amy McCroskey at Gorham Printing

Front cover picture:
A collage of pictures of Dorothy Anne Hobson as a young girl and young lady

Back cover:
An endorsement and picture of former U.S. Senator and Oregon Governor, Mark O. Hatfield

INTRODUCTION

Muscular Northwest loggers of the early 1900's wielded eight-foot long, two-man, razor-sharp saws to slash through immense stands of ancient Douglas firs. Misery whips they called their tools of the forest, slender steel bands with deep-cutting teeth powered at each end by a husky logger. Before power machines, their brute strength alone harvested Northwest timber in those early days of logging. Rigged out in grungy long johns and black denim trousers stagged at the calf, these men of the forest felled those huge old-growth trees, balancing precariously at the undercuts on narrow, metal-tipped, wooden springboards.

In the backwoods of Oregon's Little Luckiamute River, loggers initially harvested low-land trees closest to the mills. When this convenient source of green timber was depleted, voracious sawmill appetites demanded that lumbermen of the era begin cutting their swaths up the steep slopes of the less accessible Coastal Cascade mountains.

Attaining the 1500-foot ridgeline, the loggers paused, saws and double-bitted axes perched nonchalantly on their broad shoulders. Behind them, desolation and barren hillsides marked the wake of their harvest. But down there, below them in the vast new country of the Siletz River drainage, was the limitless sea of an immense green forest. Billions of feet of virgin timber, an all-encompassing forest backdrop of never-ending giant trees, awaited the ravishment of their misery whips. Those lumbermen, standing atop the ridge and viewing all that timber in the Siletz valley, probably felt akin to kids in a candy store. All they had to do was figure out how to get those magnificent trees to market.

Physical strength of men and domesticated animals moved logs from woodlands to mills during the early days of logging. Horses and oxen often struggled ponderous tree-sections to water transport—the sole means way back then of moving raw material to millsites.

Nine-year old Dorothy Anne Hobson, (right) and her first Assistant Editor, Nellie Hendrickson at work at their editorial desk during early days on the Valsetz Star, circa 1938. (Photo courtesy Graham family)

The advent of steam to the woods became the boon for Pacific Northwest timber companies where rain forests grew trees too monstrous to handle without machine power. Huge old-growth Douglas firs often exceeded ten-feet in diameter, their treetops stretching 200-feet into the rain-laden clouds. Steam boilers were capable of operating massive cable apparatus (donkey) reels to gather up logs from where they were cut, to a central point for loading onto railroad flat cars. Next they were transported by steam locomotives to the mills.

Two lumbermen from Cadillac, Michigan had bought up various homesteader's timber rights in the Siletz basin during the early 1900's. Jonathan Cobbs and William Mitchell expanded their Great Lakes enterprise to Oregon where they operated a sawmill in the small community of Hoskins, south of Falls City, about eighty miles southwest of Portland. In 1910 a devastating forest fire blazed a path of destruction through the area, singeing nearly 4,000 acres of Cobbs & Mitchell's holdings. While the burned-over forest was still merchantable, the timber barons moved men and equipment into the Siletz basin in 1912.

Rail transportation was necessary to move logs to the C & M mill in Hoskins so a railroad was immediately constructed up the Luckiamute River and into the Siletz country.

The two Michigan men, astute as they were, recognized the value of the tremendous storehouse of standing timber in the basin. A few years later Cobbs & Mitchell decided it would be more profitable to move the lumber processing facility closer to the raw material, rather than vice versa. Construction of a sawmill and housing for employees began in 1919 beside the south fork of the Siletz River. This move eliminated the 14-mile daily rail commute to Hoskins for logs and workers. A name was needed for the railroad, the rapidly growing townsite, and the mill on the river. The developers combined the name of the location—Siletz valley—and so the town of Valsetz, Oregon came into being.

C & M dammed the Siletz River to form a king-size millpond covering 377-acres with 5.5 miles of shoreline at the town's elevation of 1,100-feet. Rail spur lines were built into adjoining canyons to transport logs from the landings and cold-decks to the millpond, now dubbed Lake Valsetz.

The average annual rainfall of 140-inches in the valley assured there was seldom a shortage of water in the river or the lake. A record 187-inches—nearly 16-feet—drenched the area in 1957.

The Valsetz mill turned its first saw in 1922. By then the town's population had grown to about 300, mostly loggers and millworkers living in bachelor bunkhouses. By 1940 the population had doubled as C & M built many one-family homes allowing employees to move their wives and kids into the isolated forest community. A dead-end driving road was scrabbled out of the steep hillsides 16-miles east to the nearest civilization in Falls City. Initially the narrow road became a quagmire in winter, a dusty track in summer. Later, it was widened and gravelled which eased commuter's white-knuckle driving experiences.

Valsetz became the town at the end of the road. For anyone arriving, the isolated community had to have been the planned destination—nobody was just passing through on a journey to somewhere else. Residents soon developed a "stick-together," clannish type of community. Strangers, and they soon realized who they were, were looked upon with a certain suspicion. A friendly "hello" was often met with a stare from locals that seemed to ask, "Well, what are you doing in our town?"

In the 1920-30 era loggers were paid on average, $5.00 for a 12-hour workday. A certain rivalry developed between loggers—bush rats—and millworkers—sliver pickers.

The Valsetz post office began distributing mail in 1920.

Zip-coding officially validated the town's existence as 97393 on the postal map.

As families developed and more youngsters called Valsetz home, a school was built in 1929 for teaching the 3-R's. Later, a dormitory for teacher housing was constructed. A modern K-12 facility replaced the original school in 1981. It was rated one of the best schools in Oregon.

The town's main street was Cadillac Avenue, named for the Michigan hometown of the developers/owners. Other streets were Brownjohn, Snooseville, Shanghai, Snob Hill and Tin Can Alley.

Snob Hill was about 20-feet higher in elevation and was mostly reserved for company officials and bosses.

During the shortages of WWII the mill worked three shifts turning out millions of board-feet of lumber for the nation's war effort. Vying for top recognition in the nation, Oregon had earlier been acclaimed as the preeminent lumber producing state in the U.S.

The Valsetz townsite had now grown to about 1.5-miles long and 100-yards wide beside the river. A second housing section, named appropriately, Western, was built 1.5-miles west of the main town.

Herbert A. Templeton, President of Templeton Lumber Co., had brokered Valsetz lumber for years to firms across the nation, plus several foreign countries. In essence, he never met a Valsetz 2 X 4 he didn't like. In 1947 Cobbs & Mitchell sold Valsetz to Templeton, lock, stock and choo-choo. He purchased the mill, railroad, and the town which included 160 company, one-family houses, 30 four-man bunkhouses, store, garages and timber. His purchase included 30,000-acres of forest lands. Prior to the sale in 1947, Cobbs & Mitchell had logged about two-thirds of the Siletz basin during their 35-year reign.

In 1948 Templeton constructed a recreation hall housing the cafe, store, post office and bowling alley. The new building became "news central" and the social hub of Valsetz where many of the residents met informally to discuss recent happenings around town, and on the "outside," plus, it was rumored, an abundant quantity of local gossip.

The town was bustling in the early 1950's with 260 mill employees, 125 loggers and a total population of nearly 1,100 people.

The first T-V set arrived in Valsetz in 1953 and soon antennas sprouted on nearly every house in town. Residents reported this new form of entertainment drastically reduced the evening socializing at the rec hall.

In 1957 Templeton converted the Valsetz sawmill to plywood veneer production. Two years later he sold the whole shebang and merged it with the Boise-Cascade Corporation. Valsetz had come under the management of the third owner since its inception. Boise-Cascade owned and operated Valsetz for 25-years. Steam gave way to diesel in 1978 as the railroad was dismantled and logs were hauled to the mill on behemoth, off-road diesel powered log trucks.

During the early 1980's the supply of 150-year, old-growth timber for which the plywood mill had been built was nearly depleted. Peeling the predominant second-growth logs for veneer was quite inefficient. The mill was obliged to buy high-priced government timber which would not allow the isolated forest operation to be competitive with plywood production in the southern United States.

In 1984 Boise-Cascade announced the Valsetz mill would be closed, the town and all buildings would be demolished, burnt, and Douglas fir seedlings planted on the site. News of the impending closure, and especially the "scorched earth" strategy was met with considerable trepidation from many Valsetz residents. Some had spent their entire lives in the forest community.

Families began moving out of Valsetz seeking employment opportunities on the "outside." As a home was vacated, giant logging cats and log-loaders moved in to demolish the structure and the debris was set afire. Witnessing one home after another burnt to the ground with ensuing clouds of dense smoke created a feeling of anguish and sorrow among remaining residents. For health, and possibly emotional well-being, the burning of homes was soon held in abeyance. But eventually all homes and buildings, including the mill, were put to the torch. The charred remains were bulldozed and young tree seedlings were planted over the extinct town. And so, the 75-year life of Valsetz ended by fire, much as it had begun, rising from fire and ashes that resulted from the disastrous forest burn of 1910.

PREFACE

The Cobbs & Mitchell Lumber Company cookhouse and dormitory were operated by a hard-working, pioneer Oregon couple, Mr. and Mrs. Henry Hobson. They raised one youngster, blonde, vivacious Dorothy Anne, a young lady possessing a remarkable intellect and amazing talent well beyond her years.

When Dorothy was a nine-year-old sprite, she was sitting dwarfed in the immense C & M cookhouse dining hall one day in 1937 where she often took her meals with the rough and tumble loggers and millworkers. Before she could finish her spuds and gravy, Dorothy was joined by a family friend, Herbert A. Templeton of the Valsetz Lumber Co. In a tiny, cherubic voice she announced to Templeton that she was going to edit a newspaper for Valsetz.

With a twinkle in his eye, the lumberman put down his knife and fork and offered to be the publisher of Dorothy's newspaper. He probably assumed the make-believe project would be of short duration, if at all, and the little girl would soon go back to her dolls. But dolls were not in Dorothy's business plan, not even for a minute.

The diminutive novice editor wrote the articles for her newspaper with a stubby wooden pencil and gave the rough copy to Templeton who passed it along to his Portland-based office staff. They typed the copy as received, making no corrections in spelling, composition or subject matter. The newspaper, titled by Dorothy Anne, *The Valsetz Star*, was printed on 8½ X 14 mimeographed sheets by Templeton's office staff.

Not a make-believe, fairy tale project by any criteria, *The Star* was published monthly for four years, missing a publication date only a time or two when Dorothy was sidetracked from normal childhood maladies. Her clever witticisms, down home tell-it-like-it-is style and remarkable grasp of local and national events endeared the young, pint-sized, editor to readers everywhere. *The Star* became an overnight success with an immediate circle of enthusiastic readers. Her wordsmithing prowess indicated this nine-year-old was well past creative writing 101.

Dorothy's beguiled readers chuckled over a couple of excerpts from the *Star*'s columns in 1938:

"Russia and Finland stopped fighting but the cats are still fighting under our house something fierce.

We forgot to mention last month that we have no police or sheriff in Valsetz. Everyone just does what they please."

Aware of the entertainment value and excellent p.r. for Valsetz, not to mention benefits to his depression-beleaguered lumber sales, Herbert Templeton began mailing copies of the newspaper to lumber dealers around the nation, and several foreign countries. Dorothy Anne ran cutesy little ads in each edition, promoting Valsetz lumber. The young businesswoman recognized the value in the lumberman's silent partnership.

In *The Star*'s May, 1940 edition:

"Hurry and get your order in for Cobbs & Mitchell's nice smooth lumber. It's going fast but it's not too late if you order now."

The United States was suffering through another crippling Depression in the late 1930's—almost as severe as the devastating monetary crash of 1929. Additionally, war clouds loomed on the European skies as Germany's Adolph Hitler began his conquering march through the Balkan countries, while eyeing the British Isles with a coveting sneer of Teutonic contempt.

People were searching for an escape from the dreary news of the world—even timber people in their own Oregon backyard. *The Valsetz Star* became an enjoyable alternative to the doom and gloom headlines of the metropolitan newspapers.

The Star's "local news" column, reported in the third issue, December, 1937:

"We believe in Hemlock, Fir, Kindness, and Republicans."

(Dorothy's capital letters were for vigorous accentuation.) "We want our paper to stand for something, so we had a meeting, and we will stand for Kindness. Also, we are a Republican paper, but we will not charge democrats any more for a copy than Republicans."

(The young editor carried forth the Hobson family's strong Republican tradition. She chided Democrats by sometimes spelling the party with a lower case "d" while spelling Republican with a capital "R".)

Word of the isolated logging community's newspaper and its outspoken, pre-teen-age editor,

Dorothy Anne Hobson as she sat at her editorial desk in the Valsetz Star's editorial office in her playhouse. (Photo courtesy Graham family)

swept the Pacific Northwest, and soon the nation. More than a dozen major newspapers, from the *Portland Oregonian* to the *Denver Post* and *Christian Science Monitor*, to the *New York Herald-Tribune* and *Washington D.C Post* carried excerpts from the Valsetz *Star*. With the help of the nation's news wire services, Dorothy Anne was fast becoming a national personality, while putting the name of the backwoods timber town on everybody's map.

As her fame spread across the country, the impish editor was congratulated by many celebrities for her honest, outspoken and satirical writings in *The Star*. Dorothy wrote in the May, 1940 edition:

"We received a letter from Shirley Temple and she thinks editing a paper would be fun—but it isn't."

Nearly as far away from Valsetz as it's possible to get in the continental U.S., Miami radio station WOAM quoted Dorothy Anne's writings over their airwaves.

Mrs. Franklin D. Roosevelt, with a well-deserved chuckle, quoted *The Star* at her regular press conference in Washington D.C. Other notables who wrote to Dorothy included: Kate Smith (through her press agent), Postmaster General James Farley, Herbert Hoover, Wendell Willkie (who ran for U.S. President on the Republican ticket in 1940.), and his Vice- Presidential nominee, U.S. Senator from Oregon, Charles L. McNary. The Republicans loved this little lady. As Dorothy herself would have put it, "Some democrats did too."

The congratulatory outpouring from across the country didn't turn the head of the young Valsetz editor. She continued to ramrod the newspaper from its editorial office in her playhouse behind the lumber company-furnished family home. Dorothy lost her first assistant editor through a move out of town during the early publishing days. But she developed her alter ego in Franklin Thomas, a Valsetz youngster of about her own age and laudable maturity, who she appointed Assistant Editor early in 1938.

Much credit for the young lady's prowess must be conferred upon her parents, Henry and Ruby Hobson. They reportedly were avid readers and often sat down with their only offspring discussing world events and factual topics gleaned from their readings.

In addition to her jabs at Democrats, Adolph Hitler, and Valsetz rain, Dorothy Anne also showed her serious side. *The Star*'s third issue, the 1937 Christmas edition, contained a nostalgic, well-composed little ditty titled, "Life in a Lumber Town."

"We think it is lots of fun to live in a mountain lumber town.
The air is fine, and it's a thrill when the logs come bounding down.
The ladies all play bridge at night, and sometimes in the day.
But we roller skate and sing and tap, to pass the time away."

Dorothy Anne Hobson published the monthly Valsetz *Star* for four years, almost fifty issues. Her publishing benefactor, Herbert A. Templeton, stayed with her the entire time, as did her second Assistant Editor, Franklin Thomas.

Without advance notice, the young lady editor, now a venerable newspaper tycoon at thirteen, abruptly announced the *Star*'s forthcoming demise with the December, 1941 issue. Perhaps the timing was most fortuitous at year-end—maybe subscriptions expired in December, and Dorothy didn't want loyal subscribers to feel short-changed. Regardless of the reason, she closed the playhouse door and wrote "finis" to *The Valsetz Star* with that final Christmas issue. Ironically, it was also the month which launched the U.S. entry into WWII via the Japanese sneak attack on Pearl Harbor.

Upon closing shop, Dorothy said she would be going to Salem's Parrish Junior High School to, "improve her education, take music and vocal lessons, and have her teeth straightened, with no time left for anything except the Parrish Pep Club."

Dorothy Anne Hobson was an amazingly talented and determined young lady who envisioned a seemingly unattainable goal, then bolstered sagging spirits of her depressed and news-weary readers through an inspired and entertaining journalism adventure.

* * * * * *

In 1942, Herbert A. Templeton, President of the Templeton Lumber Co., and longtime Portland philanthropist, wrote this introduction to articles about Dorothy Anne and Valsetz:

"'There's going to be a newspaper in Valsetz,' said nine year old Dorothy Anne Hobson. It was in the fall of 1937. We two were having a late lunch at the cookhouse table an hour after the mill crew had eaten and gone. 'Who's going to be the editor?' I queried. 'I am,' replied Dorothy Anne, 'would you like to see the first paper?' So up came a school scratch pad which she thumbed over to a page headed in large print, '*The Valsetz Star*,' and began reading to me the editor's notes—local news—school doings, etc. It was at once apparent that the editor was able. Valsetz surely offered a good and fertile field. Why shouldn't Valsetz have a paper? A deal was promptly consummated whereby our Portland office, splendidly equipped with a sixty-dollar mimeograph outfit, would print *The Valsetz Star*. Dorothy Anne chose to dignify us with the title of publishers.

Valsetz is the home of the Cobbs & Mitchell sawmill operation, situated just a few miles west of the divide in the Coast Range mountains near the headwaters of the Siletz River, eighty miles southwest of Portland. It is a very isolated spot, being accessible only by the Valley and Siletz railroad connecting with the Southern Pacific main line at Independence, forty-four miles away; and a winding mountain dirt road which is impassable during the winter months each year. Dorothy Anne is the daughter of Mr. and Mrs. Henry Hobson, who run the company cookhouse and dormitory system. All her life, Dorothy Anne has sat down to breakfast, dinner and supper with a hundred or more husky sawmill men and loggers. From babyhood she was the undoubted cookhouse favorite, but fortunately her association and popularity with the men only served to sharpen her quick wits, without spoiling her. The only schooling until just now, when she is going to Salem (Parrish) Junior High, has been in the Valsetz public schools, along with the children of other company employees. She has had, however the inestimable advantage of highly intelligent parents who read every good book they can lay their hands on, all the worthwhile periodicals, listen to the best of the radio, and then discuss interestingly and pithily what they have read and heard. Of all the dinner tables I know, for interesting, worthwhile conversation, give me the cookhouse table at Valsetz when the cookhouse crew sit down with Henry and Mrs. Hobson opposite each other at the head of the table.

When the first issue of *The Star* came off the press, the Valsetz allotment was promptly sold out at 2¢ a copy, and a hundred or so copies went to a list from our office; two or three lumber trade journals; our sales representatives; a few customers and a few personal friends here and there. The second issue came out and then response began to roll in to Editor Dorothy Anne. People liked *The Star* and wanted more of it. Trade journals carried stories on it. One large daily editor wrote Dorothy Anne a corking letter welcoming her to the fraternity of American newspapers, but warning her against invasion of his circulation territory. A man from Kansas City—where he picked up a copy, I don't know—sent her a dollar with a letter explaining that he hoped that might be the price of a year's subscription, and would she please list his name accordingly. In the next issue Dorothy Anne mentioned the incident, and then the dollar subscriptions began to roll in. That's another unique thing about *The Star*. It had two circulation lists. One from our office, free to anyone who cared to ask for it, and one from Dorothy Anne's office at a dollar a year. Her circulation was soon more than twice as large as ours.

And so *The Star* continued through four years until the fall of 1941, when out of a clear sky (seldom found in Valsetz) without either asking or receiving counsel from her publishers, the editor calmly announced that she would discontinue at the end of the year. In those four years Dorothy Anne has become a national figure, with subscribers and friends in nearly every state of the union, as well as South America, Hawaii and the Philippines. At least a score of large daily papers throughout the country from New York to San Francisco carried stories on her. Her mail grew to rather overwhelming proportions. Forty-two letters came from New York and vicinity alone in one mail.

We later discovered that on the preceding Sunday the 'New York Herald-Tribune' had carried a full column story and large picture of Dorothy Anne. Mrs. Roosevelt read a copy of *The Star* before her press conference and the next day the A.P. and U.P. wire services carried the story of *The Star* to every corner of the land.

But, in the following pages you will read *The Valsetz Star* and discover for yourself why Dorothy Anne was acclaimed throughout the land and hailed editorially by the *'Eugene Register-Guard'* as 'Oregon's most widely known and most useful editor.'"

Herbert A. Templeton

Writers–East and West
Autumn–November 6, 1937

On November 3, 1937, the First Lady of the land, Mrs. Eleanor Roosevelt, wife of U.S. Democratic President, Franklin D. Roosevelt, made a public appearance at Harper & Brothers for the debut of her new book, *"This is My Story."*

Three days later in the tiny, remote logging town of Valsetz, Oregon, Dorothy Anne Hobson also launched her first literary work. *The Valsetz Star*, a monthly one-page, mimeographed newspaper for and about the forest residents, sold for two-cents, or you could have it delivered by mail for a dollar a year.

Strangely enough, the two writers, from opposite ends of the nation, later became acquainted through the mail. Mrs. Roosevelt chuckled at Dorothy Anne's satire as she read from *The Star* at a weekly press conference in Washington D.C. The diminutive editor, although a staunch Republican supporter from a long line of Oregon Republicans, respected and admired Eleanor Roosevelt. She later wrote, "Mrs. Roosevelt scrubs her face with Sweetheart soap every night."

Morale Booster
Autumn–November 25, 1937

The tall timber in the Siletz River basin is bountifully nourished by Oregon's abundant rainfall. The coastal range of mountains, soaring to a height of nearly 3,500-feet initially catch the rain-laden clouds sloshing easterly off the stormy Pacific Ocean. Bumping the coastal peaks unleashes the record rainfall for which the area is renowned.

Life was dreary for most Valsetz residents especially during the rainy season, jokingly identified by some as lasting from January lst to December 31st. Excluding a few dry weeks during the brief summer when dirt turned to dust, locals learned to live with the ubiquitous mud. It was everywhere—sucking at boots and shoes, splattering cars and clothing, even dogs and cats became lathered with the brownish goo. One can imagine the looks of the woebegone loggers traipsing home after a wickedly wet day in the woods.

Dorothy Anne attempted to be Valsetz' primary morale booster for the dispirited residents of the rain-drenched forest community. The Star's monthly publication day became a celebratory event in the otherwise lackluster life of the villagers, especially during the extended rainy season. Her impish portrayal of local happenings, intertwined with a certain tricycle-type of humor uplifted local spirits while entertaining *The Star's* readers across the nation.

*   *   *   *   *   *

Nobody in Valsetz seemed to care, but Hollywood actress Marlene Dietrich's legs made her the highest paid woman in the world.

The Thanksgiving weather forecast in *The Star* still predicted rain until December 25th.

The elfin editor tritely wrote:
"Mr. Paul: 'There's the mill whistle. It's blowing for the fire.'
Cliff Frazer: 'No it isn't, it's blowing for the water. They've already got the fire.'"

Under Special Editor's Note, Dorothy Anne had this dire comment: "This may be our last issue as we are going broke. We have to pay out so much money. We have to pay our publishers in Portland, and we have to buy stamps and paper. Daddy says the Republicans could save us but there aren't any. My Mother says we could all do nothing for an hour like they do in the cook house.

Mr. Starr told us to keep struggling, but Nellie who helps me with the paper says she is getting tired of struggling as we haven't divided up the money yet. I have it all but we will divide it before Christmas."

"Things to be thankful for this Thanksgiving Day: That our living room only leaks in one corner instead of all over.
That the new truck road didn't slide into the pond."

<u>Things</u> <u>Of</u> <u>Interest</u>
A <u>Poem</u>

We only wish the sky would clear for Cobbs & Mitchell here.
We hope the men won't go away, and so we think that we shall pray
That we can work and get things done, and so, dear Lord, please let us run."
(There was no explanation for the concern expressed.)

"Mr. Templeton is a very kind man. He is helping us by publishing our paper. He has not asked for any money yet but we think he will the next time he comes up. We will not have much for Xmas if he wants his pay. Everybody says he is a very kind man." (Flattery will get you everything)

"President Roosevelt is going to employ everybody and Ann Heydon (Valsetz Postmaster) is helping him."

"On Tuesdays after school we have secret meetings as we are making Xmas presents for our parents."

"Mr. Thomas hopes things are getting better and Mr. Starr says they are getting worse and Mr. Mitchell went back to Michigan."

"Mrs. Grout gave an especially nice party in honor of Miss Cecil Thomas. They played contract. A guest prize was given to Miss Thomas who is a very charming dark lady from St. Paul."

"June Kackley, daughter of Engineer Kackley, is a new seventh grade pupil. We think she is lovely."

SOUNDS AND SMELLS
AUTUMN–DECEMBER, 1937

During its heyday, the town of Valsetz shared its uniqueness with very few other Northwest communities. Where else could one find an isolated, end-of-road location with logging and sawmill alike, families living in comfortable homes, kids attending first-class, accredited in-town K-12 schooling, daily passenger rail system, local store and services including, for heaven's sake, a bowling alley? And the whole megillah owned by an understanding employer like Cobbs & Mitchell. The Simpson Timber Company's Camp Grisdale, in the Olympic Mountains of Western Washington, would have become Valsetz' nearest clone.

Former residents of the tiny forest community that was tucked beneath the western face of Oregon's Coastal mountain range mostly agreed that the people made Valsetz a good place to live. They enjoyed the camaraderie, knowing their neighbors could be depended upon in time of need.

The sounds and smells of the logging/lumber operation linger faintly in the storehouse of memories retained by a nostalgic few. Throughout town was heard the constant whine of the saws at the mill biting into immense fir logs, not at once a comforting sound but something habit-forming and a silence abruptly alerted when they stopped.

The hissing of steam and its accompanying aroma was every-

Dorothy Anne Hobson in her younger, pre-Valsetz Star days, astride her pony, "Val." (Photo courtesy Graham family)

where; train engines, huge donkey boilers, mill equipment pushing, pulling and lifting by means of harnessed superheated water. And a smell like nothing else; moist, warm and pleasant to the senses with a faint hint of fresh wood fibers.

Daily, the trains brought their loads of behemoth logs to the town's mill pond where the sounds of unloading reverberated throughout the village. The chugging of the donkey engine tipping the loads, then the swish of water as the once proud forest monarchs momentarily slid nobly beneath the surface. And everywhere was the smell of grease and oil, lubricants and fuel essential to the mechanization associated with wood manufacturing.

But, perhaps the sweetest smell of all was found out of town, away from man's manufactured odors. A short walk into the forest brought the aromas of nature—saturated fir boughs on a soggy morning, pungent smells of pitch oozing from spruce and hemlock bark, logged hillsides of summer's fragrant fireweed and the varied berry plant fragrances that emanate from the dense underbrush beneath the forest canopy.

These are the memories of Valsetz residents, remembrances of never again.

*   *   *   *   *   *

Back in Valsetz, Dorothy Anne initially appointed a school chum, Nellie Hendrickson, as her Assistant-Editor of *The Star*. Nellie's name appeared on the newspaper's masthead early on, as she began helping Dorothy with the editorial duties of the community's monthly editions. The Hendrickson family moved out of Valsetz in 1938 and the diminutive editor chose another school friend, Franklin Thomas as her new Assistant-Editor.

Dorothy's December, 1937 issue had the same dreary weather forecast as before, albeit somewhat abbreviated. "More Rain."

"Merry Christmas to all our readers! We believe in Hemlock, Fir, Kindness, and Republicans. There will be something in this corner every month. We want our paper to stand for something, so we had a meeting, (Dorothy and Nellie) and we will stand for kindness. Also we are a Republican paper, but we will not charge democrats any more for a copy than Republicans."

"Business is getting a little better. We sold all our November papers, only one man didn't pay us. He read the paper and said it wasn't any good. So we are going to write to Mr. Starr, the Cobbs & Mitchell General Manager, and have him collect our money. Mr. Starr is a lawyer, and he tells us who is right, and who is wrong."

"We will try to have a poem every issue. Sometimes it won't be very good, as we have trouble making the words rhyme."

"Sometimes we wish Mr. Clancy was here to help us. He was editor of the '*Valsetz Spotlight*' last year. He had lots of good ideas like *The Oregonian*."

"There is a beautiful Xmas tree in the Cobbs & Mitchell store window, and lots of gifts to buy. We hope everybody will buy, as Mr. Grout who manages the store does not like a lot of things left over to send back."

"Falls City basketball team beat Valsetz team 24 to 4. Star players on the Valsetz team were Bill McCoy and Billy Frazer."

"We had a letter from the Assistant Editor of the *The Seattle Times*, and he likes our paper. Also, Mr. Boettinger, of the *Seattle Post-Intellingencer* is President Roosevelt's son-in-law, read our paper, and wrote us a very nice letter. We hope he will not mind us being Republicans. We think President Roosevelt has a kind smile, and Mrs. Roosevelt helps poor people, but we can't change—all our grandfathers were Republicans—two Nellie's and one mine."

"We also had a nice letter from 'The Timberman', 'American Lumberman', Mr. L.G. Knight, of 'Bethlehem Steel Company', 'Saunders Lumber Co.' of Nebraska, and several others."

"We are going to study more about lumber, and learn the difference between Fir and Hemlock, and then we may raise the price of our paper. Mr. Boettinger told us in his letter to raise the price of our paper. Some of the kids at school said we never got a letter fro Mr. Boettinger, but we invited them over to my playhouse where we have our office in the corner and now they know; but Mr. Templeton is the cause of it all. He knows people all over the world and sends them our paper and then they write to us."

"Valsetz has a population of eight hundred people, with 205 school children. We have seven very nice teachers."

"The school is giving a fine Xmas program, and there will be a big community tree and lots of candy."

HISTORY
WINTER–JANUARY, 1938

Early settlers were known to have wandered into the Siletz drainage country during the mid-1800's. James Nesmith powwowed with Siletz Indians along the river as early as 1849. In 1856 a fort was constructed at Hoskins in King's Valley southeast of Valsetz. It was garrisoned by the army to protect settlers from Indians, but abandoned for lack of business a decade later.

Hardy homesteaders staked claims in the five-mile wide Siletz basin, including Oscar Fanno who claimed 160-acres beside a creek that flowed into the Siletz River at what would become the Valsetz townsite. Fanno's name was later given to several landmarks in the basin, the creek by his homestead cabin and the towering mountain ridge that smiled down onto his holdings.

Most settlers were farmers but the land was not suitable for agriculture because it was forested with those pesky trees which had to be cut down and burned before crop cultivation could begin. In those days the forest was of little value except for building shelter and cooking vittles after a hard day of work sawing down the dratted things. Little did the homesteaders know the forest they blasphemed would one day become vertical, green spires of gold.

Land grants were awarded to homesteaders around the turn of the century and in quick succession speculators, betting on the future value of the timber, easily bought up various parcels of land from settlers in the basin. Timbermen Jonathan Cobbs and his partner William Mitchell from Cadillac, Michigan acquired 36,000 acres of Siletz timber from speculators prior to a forest fire that swept the region in 1910. It was decided to log the singed trees while the timber was still merchantable, earlier than originally planned. Railroad construction to transport logs to the sawmills in Hoskins and Falls City began in 1912, with the rails arriving at the Valsetz townsite five years later.

From that time forward the region has supplied timber to Oregon's economy for each of more than eighty-years.

*　*　*　*　*　*

Dorothy Anne's Valsetz *Star* changed the weather forecast in January's issue: "Rain till the Fourth of July."

"We are studying current events in the fourth grade, and the country needs more houses."

"We heard President Roosevelt's Jackson Day speech, and he said the White House door was open. Nellie and I wish we lived closer so we could go in. There is a dog there who is ninety-six inches long and has a four-inch tail. Nellie's dog is very short."

"Our publishers in Portland are Miss Richards and Miss Heimbucher. Both work in Mr. Templeton's office. Of course we can't be sure they won't strike. We are going to send them some chocolate fudge."

"ADVERTISEMENT: Go to Mrs. Spray's Beauty Parlor for a permanent wave, and Fred Shaad will fix your shoes."

"A POEM
There's lots of trouble round about, But we think it's best to smile.
Not much use to grump around with a long face all the while.
Most folks love a happy face, it cheers them far and near;
And another thing it does for us, wipes out that old man fear."

"Mr. Thomas, our superintendent, was in Portland about his business. Mr. McLean, our logging superintendent, goes to work in the

dark, comes home in the dark, and never says a word."

"In geography we are studying about France. They have many beautiful cathederals and they owe us some money."

"Ann B. Heydon, who is our postmistress, has an autographed photograph of Mr. James Farley. She met him in an elevator in San Francisco."

"Nellie Hendrickson, the Assistant Editor, thinks she will give up newspaper work—she thinks she would like the movies. She

Dorothy Anne and her mother, Ruby Hobson, dressed in their summer finery. (Photo courtesy Graham family)

has big brown eyes and curly hair. My eyes are blue, and my hair is straight. Mrs. Roosevelt wrote a book, and she was plain too. We have the book."

"Mr. Templeton wrote to a lumber company in New Jersey, and said he had his eye on the rainbow and a rabbit's foot in his pocket. Nellie and I laughed and laughed—we don't know what he meant. He looks serious, but he isn't."

"We do not have to worry about going broke any more. Even after we said we were Republicans, we sold lots of papers. One Republican wrote and said we must stick together, and save the country, so we have a small amount of money put away in case the Republicans need our help."

"Our staff artist is Mrs. Al Lang who works in the dining room. She is very clever."

"Mr. Templeton left with Mrs. Templeton for a trip to California to sell *The Valsetz Star*. Mr. Templeton is also president of the Templeton Lumber Company, but he may give up the Portland lumber business. (?To sell *The Valsetz Star* at 2¢ per copy??)"

AUSTRIA INVADED
WINTER–MARCH, 1938

(There was not a February, 1938 issue.)

On March 12, 1938, the simmering European war became a boiling cauldron of aggression as Adolph Hitler's German Panzer army swept into Austria without firing a shot. Two days later Hitler victoriously goose-stepped his way into the historic city of Vienna. His storm-troopers were busily engaged teaching Austrians the reprehensible Nazi salute.

Earlier that year, Great Britain's foreign secretary, Anthony Eden, had resigned over a disagreement with his government. As the British people witnessed Germany's aggression just a few miles away across the Channel, many thought the political upheaval within their own government had resulted from serious disagreements on neutrality between English hawks and doves.

Meanwhile, in Valsetz, Dorothy and her fourth-grade companions were studying about World Goodwill Day when children around the globe were being urged to join together in peaceful friendship.

In Valsetz, *The Star* reported the month's weather forecast: "Fair and warmer."

"The price of The Valsetz *Star* is still only 2¢ per copy, or one dollar per year by mail."

"Nellie Hendrickson, the Assistant Editor will not give up news-paper work for awhile, as we read an article and Hollywood is full."

"We had a letter from a young man in Germany whose father is a lumberman. He read about our paper in *The Timberman* magazine. We will print the letter so all our subscribers can read it. But you will have to get Mr. Lewis Shunke, Otto Ganton, and Fred Shaad to help you. We did!"

"Nellie and I went for a long walk so we could talk over big ques-tions for our paper, like the trouble in China, and Mr. Eden getting mad, and Hitler standing so straight in his high boots and leather belt, talking to the people, but we don't understand about any of it. We hope our readers won't mind. We had a lovely walk, and the sun was shining and the pussy willows were out, and everyone we passed was singing, 'Whistle While You Work.' We think people are happy in Valsetz."

"Mr. Templeton was going to give up the lumber business and sell The *Star* but he only made thirty-cents selling *The Star* so he is going to keep the lumber business."

"The people had a surprise on Mr. Grout on his 39th birthday. They came to his home in Locust Drive with a white cake with yel-low candles. He was surprised but he didn't say much."

"Mrs. Ann B. Heydon, who lives high got locked in her apart-ment. She screamed and Jody Rhodes came. He had a ladder."

"People whom we think are going to be married. We aren't sure but they are: Kenny Goins, Vincent Ryan, Joe Girler, Jingles."

"Mr. and Mrs. Charles T. Mitchell and Mr. and Mrs. Kaiser, from Cadillac, Michigan, spent two days in Valsetz. Mrs. Kaiser loves hot cakes, cookies and cats. They have gone to bathe in Honolulu."

We have many clubs in Valsetz: The Ladies Aid Sewing Club, the Bridge Club, Athletic Club, 4-H Club, Boy Scouts, Camp Fire Girls, Rod and Gun Club, and the Union."

WAR CLOUDS
SPRING–APRIL, 1938

In several 1938 editions of *The Star*, Dorothy and her Assistant Editor mentioned concerns of the people in the Northwest about the war that was simmering in Europe. Most residents realized that Germany, seemingly far away, was but an ocean removed from the U.S. east coast. Pearl Harbor was still 3½-years away but the Japanese war machine had already committed atrocities against China. At this time in history, both Germany and Japan were mobilizing men and materiel, preparing to attack their peaceful, defenseless neighbors.

In 1938, the nation was divided between those who favored U.S. involvement into the European clash, vs. people who felt we should remain neutral—hawks vs. doves, war mongers against isolationists. As more evidence of aggression and brutality by Germany and Japan became known, the tide of opinion would favor U.S. support of nations attempting to resist Germany's ruthless dictator, Adolph Hitler.

In Valsetz, Dorothy Anne was doing her bit to ease the growing tensions between Germany and America through friendly correspondence.

* * * * * *

And in Valsetz, Dorothy Anne reported:

"Following is the letter written in English which we received from Mr. Seigfried Vogel, of Germany. We printed it last month written in German.

Dear Little Miss:

I have just seen your picture in *The Timberman of Portland*, which I received today. I am 20-years old. My father is a lumberman and I have undertaken to follow the same calling. I should very much like to correspond in order to learn and perfect English correspondence.

Before writing again I should like to be certain that this is the right address.

My father was for many years in East Asia in quite a large sawmill operation, in particular, Shanghai. Also in Australia. Upon hearing from you I shall immediately write again.

> With best German greetings,
> also to your dear parents,
> *Seigfried Vogel*"

"We had a Republican meeting and nobody came, but we think we will have a bigger crowd the next time."

"We had a letter from Mr. Glen Rice of Kansas City. He sent us a dollar, but he forgot to enclose it. He is a democrat. He said the Republicans couldn't think and that they had passed out, but Daddy said some of the Democrats had passed out too."

"May the 15th to the 21st is National Air Mail Week. Send lots of letters. Write to your girl friend and your boy friend, and your grandmother. Buy air mail stamps from Mrs. Ann Heydon."

"Our Sunday School Teacher and 4-H Club Leader, Mrs. Frank Morovec, is leaving Valsetz. We had a farewell birthday for her in the dining room. It was her 26th birthday. There was a big white cake with 26 candles. Mother said it must be wonderful to put the exact number of candles on a cake and think nothing of it. She is quite old."

"Fred Shaad will fix your shoes and your house, both."
"Doctor Spray will cure what's wrong with you."

"Governor Martin of Oregon calls some people 'Goons.' Nellie and I laughed. We looked it up in the dictionary. It isn't there."

"We hope all our teachers will come back next term of school, especially Mrs. Williamson, who is our fourth grade teacher."

"Local News and Things of Interest.
Mrs. Ann Heydon, our post mistress, may leave for Czechoslovakia to save her country. She has four guns. She came from there in a tight basque and full skirt. It's very hard to spell."

"In our fourth grade junior weekly reader it says the people of our country want peace. There is a picture of women and children in Spain being driven from their homes. We hope we won't have war and be driven from our homes in winter, because Mother got a new chair and lamp, and we can't get over the Valsetz road in winter time."

"Mrs. O'Reiffe does funny art in the 'Life' magazine. She had pink roses in a sow's ear."
"Mr. Wesley Appleton was injured in the logging department. Mother and I called on him at the Deaconess Hospital in Salem. We were going to get him some flowers if there was any money left from 'Snow White,' but there wasn't any. But Mother had some money left from her shoes so we got him some anyway."

"We have six Republicans on our mailing list now, and four dollars in our Republican fund."

NOTORIETY
SPRING–MAY, 1938

Six months into the newspaper publishing business, The Valsetz *Star* and Dorothy Anne were beginning to be noticed, not only in Oregon, but across the country. On May 5th, her tenth birthday, the rosy-cheeked editor was recognized by the National Library of Amateur Journalism in Philadelphia, Pennsylvania. Dorothy and her Assistant-Editor, Nellie Hendrickson also had been invited as guests of the Oregon State Legislature.

Much of *The Star*'s notoriety undoubtedly occurred from Herbert Templeton mailing the newspaper to everyone who was anyone in the lumber business. It's not known how, but the national wire services also received copies and put tidbits from *The Star* on the media wire which they perceived would make entertaining reading in newspapers across the land. After all, satirical writings from a nine-year old outspoken young lady at the helm of her own newspaper in a backwoods burgh with a strange sounding name was sure to make copy in the big city dailies. And it did.

*   *   *   *   *   *

The Star's May edition announced that May 8th had been named World Good Will Day. "It is the only day of the year that nations join together in thinking of peace. Or, at least they should. Such a day helps to make the nations of the world better friends. We didn't even quarrel at school on that day."

33

"In our Junior Weekly Reader it says that the boys and girls of the United States have made thousands of little friends in other lands, and are now sending suitcases of friendship to Spain. Each suitcase will have in it a letter of friendship written in both English and Spanish. It will also have toys, pictures and useful things, such as clothing, toothbrushes and sewing materials. On the suitcases these words are written: "Friendship and Good Will-Our Sure Defense.""

"Advertisement: Get your lumber from Cobbs & Mitchell. It's nice and smooth."

"The Republicans have a pump. It is electric."

"Mr. Henry Ford ate lunch with President Roosevelt, and Mr. Templeton ate lunch with us."

"Mrs. Max Keiser was elected president of the Parent-Teachers for next year. Mother thought she was going to get president but she is only vice-president."

"Fifty Democrats will come to Valsetz the first of June, and Mrs. Ann B. Heydon will be leading them. They all work in post offices. We are glad they are coming, but we wish they were Republicans."

"Thursday night everybody graduated at the Community Hall. It was lovely."

"The Valsetz school children attended the spring song festival at Monmouth."

"Miss Greta Garbo and Leopold Stokowski are on the Isle of Capri."

"Mrs. Roosevelt likes our Paper. She told *The New York Sun* she did."

"General Pershing is getting better. He is very brave. He and my Uncle Len fought together in France in 1918."

"The 4-H Girls Club is very busy. We are learning to make hot chocolate and milk toast. Nellie and I think we would like to be cooks. Mrs. Morovec, our instructor, is very patient while we spill things on her kitchen floor."

TEN-YEARS OLD
SUMMER–JULY, 1938

At about the same time Dorothy Anne celebrated her tenth birthday on May 5, 1938, she also had nearly completed the fourth grade in the Valsetz school—two memorable events in the life of the young editor. We would assume her parents, Henry and Ruby Hobson staged a grandiose party to honor the event with young friends, ice cream and a lip-smacking birthday cake. Surprisingly, not a birthday word was mentioned in *The Star*.

By the time she was ten-years old, this remarkable young lady from the secluded logging town in Oregon was beginning to make a name for herself, locally, and across the nation. Many celebrities and high-ranking officials chuckled at The *Star*'s entertaining and provocative excerpts.

Dorothy didn't play favorites, no indeed; often her barbless journalistic arrows were purposely launched to boomerang back to herself, her assistant, *The Star*, sometimes even her parents or school/lumber company executives. (i.e. August 1938 edition:)

"Henry Hobson (Dorothy's dad) went to Breitenbush Hot Springs

to reduce and he gained five
pounds."

Nothing or nobody was
sidestepped or sacred, with the
notable exceptions of her
country and it's flag, and her
God.

If only those exclusions
were recognized and accepted
today.

*   *   *   *   *   *

In the July, 1938 issue of
The Valsetz Star, Dorothy Anne
reported: "Weather Forecast:
Fair and Warmer."

("We didn't have a June issue of 'The Star.' School was
out, and Nellie and I played

Portland lumber executive, philanthropist, and longtime member of the Westminster Presbyterian Church, Herbert A. Templeton. The lumberman brokered Valsetz production for many years, buying out Cobbs & Mitchell in 1947. He volunteered his Portland office staff to publish the Valsetz Star during its four-years of publication. (Photo courtesy Graham family)

too much. We hope nobody wants their money back.")

"Editor's Corner: We will not say so much about Republicans in
this issue because we had some papers left over last month. Besides,
we met some awfully nice Democrats."

"Last Sunday, June 26th, fifty members of the Polk and Marion
County Postmasters' Association arrived in Valsetz to be the guests of
Mrs. Ann B. Heydon, our postmistress. They arrived in cars, and
were all here by one o' clock. Everybody contributed towards the en-

tertainment. This is the first time we have used the word 'contrib-uted,' but we will be using bigger words from now on because Mother bought the 'Book of Knowledge' set for us from Mrs. Shea of Portland, and she gave us a big dictionary with the set. We will pay for it later."

"Soon after all the Democrats arrived, they were loaded on a big company truck, with Mr. Jensen, as driver (He is a Democrat, too.) for a trip over the high Cobbs & Mitchell logging road. Mrs. Heydon and Mr. Thomas, our superintendent, went with them to explain how we got such good lumber, and about the view."

"Mr. Thomas was the only Republican on the truck, but the ladies all said he was the gayest Republican they had ever met. When the truck left he was seated with Mr. Jensen, the driver, in the front seat, but he got acquainted up on the hill and on the return trip was seated in the back in the midst of the ladies."

"Mr. McLean, our logging superintendent, made all arrangements for the trip, but he is quite bashful, and wouldn't come to the party."

"As soon as they returned from the hill trip they all went to the Cobbs & Mitchell dining room, and had turkey and speeches."

"Mr. Thomas entered the dining room with Mrs. Moses on his arm. She is very gay. Mr. Moses says funny things. He is dark and has been ill, and is postmaster in Corvallis. He took a nap in Mrs. Heydon's apartment while she was up on the hill in the truck."

"The Democrats bring their own dessert. They came with crates of fresh strawberries and a bucket of cherries."

"We wish President Roosevelt and Mr. Farley had been here. They would have had fun."

"After the dinner, there were speeches and much laughing and many jokes. President Butterfield from Woodburn gave a talk and Mrs. Wisecarver from McMinnville. She is very beautiful and wore black and white, and Mrs. May Johnson, a newspaper woman smiled and bowed, and wore pretty brown."

"Advertisement: Everybody is buying Cobbs & Mitchell lumber. Send in your order right away. Call Mr. Templeton in Portland. He will sell you some. Remember—'It's Nice and Smooth.'"

"Mr. and Mrs. Paul Miller, from Salem, sat at our table and Mr. Miller said lots of jokes. Mrs. Miller told him he was talking too much. I heard her tell him."

"After the dinner, they all went to Mother's house, escorted by Mrs. Heydon and Mr. Thomas, for a few hours of bridge. Later Mr. and Mrs. Grout dropped in for bridge and to help entertain. All together it was a happy day, and we hope they don't come again for awhile because we want to stay Republican."

"Mr. George Paul, our school principal, will leave on a trip to Chicago next week. The rest of us will stay here or else go to the beach."

"Mr. Ickes got married."

"President Roosevelt said in his fireside chat that some man is making a thousand dollars a day, but nobody here is."

FOREST FIRES
SUMMER–AUGUST, 1938

Fire is the most significant threat to Pacific Northwest forests where several major burns have occurred during the twentieth century. The damages are not only costly to the lumber industry but also cause irreplaceable losses in terms of the environment, animals and their habitat, and sometimes human lives.

The Tillamook, Oregon burn was one of the most devastating forest fires to hit the Northwest. It began on August 14, 1933, and in ten days had burned 40,000 acres. Then, almost without warning, the dozing giant of destruction erupted into a cataclysmal fire storm that mere man could not quell nor even slow down. Astoundingly, in less than twenty-four hours the ravenous flames, leaping from treetop to treetop consumed an additional 200,000 acres of prime-growth green timber. In total, eleven-billion board-feet were destroyed in the original conflagration, plus smaller Tillamook fires in 1939-45-51. One death occurred during the initial burn, and another in 1951.

The monstrous Tillamook fire sent clouds of ashes above twenty-thousand feet. Ships sailing 400-miles off the Pacific coast reported their decks were covered with the gray debris from the skies. In Tillamook itself, some residents measured two feet of ashes on their streets.

In 1948, Oregon voters authorized a $13-million bond issue to replant the barren area of the Tillamook burn. A portion was planted by Oregon schoolchildren and convict labor but 98% was completed by contracted workers.

Modernization and technology have greatly reduced the incidence and severity of forest fires. Fixed wing planes and helicopters afford faster identification, quicker response times and considerably enhanced suppression methods. Today, forest fires are located faster, fire crews get to the scene quicker and acreage loss is proportionately reduced.

Before fighting fires comes programs aimed at eliminating them entirely. Millions are spent annually on public education to teach methods and habits that stop fires before they carelessly begin. Smokey Bear is a universally-recognized symbol of prevention to young and old alike.

In September, 1936, more than sixty-percent of Bandon, an Oregon coastal town, was destroyed by a forest fire. That burn claimed the lives of eleven people. Valsetz itself came within a wisp of being wiped out by a forest fire on a dry, hot afternoon in August, 1938. When it had burned to the edge of town, a providential wind change turned the flames towards a logged-off area where they died.

In *The Star*, Dorothy tells of the fire that nearly charred the town: "The fire came roaring towards us. I saved my new pajamas and '*The Book of Knowledge,*' and Nellie saved their brown hen with the two little chickens."

*   *   *   *   *   *

The August, 1938 edition of the Valsetz *Star* gave a sure-thing weather forecast: "Rain this fall."

Under "Special Editor's Notes, Dorothy Anne reported: "We will not say so much about the Democrats in this issue because we got quite a few dollars from the Republicans and we are afraid some of them will get mad."

"The Democrats laugh a lot but they haven't much money. One man told us we couldn't have a newspaper and laugh all the time, but we like to laugh."

"Mother and I had a lovely visit at the home of the President of our publishing company, Mr. Templeton in Portland. I read Emily Post for an hour before we went and after I got there I couldn't remember any of it.

We had dinner on a terrace and a pretty maid served from the left and removed from the right, or served from the right and removed from the left, I'm not sure which, but it was perfect, and not a bit like the cookhouse at Valsetz where everybody just reaches."

"The next day Mr. Templeton wore a red rose and took seven ladies to lunch at the Portland Hotel. Later we drove out to the Swan Island Air Port and saw a big mainliner land. We went aboard and met the stewardess. She was beautiful with shining black hair and gleaming white teeth, and Mr. Templeton said she weighed exactly one hundred and ten pounds."

"Back downtown to Mr. Templeton's office where everybody was busy but Mr. Robbins. He was gazing out the window."

"We stopped at the fourth floor to visit the Cobbs & Mitchell office. Saw Betty Starr in the elevator. She sings and is attractive and wore a doll's hat."

"Also, Mr. Starr came to the door smiling and welcomed us. He held mother's hand quite a while! Mr. Mitchell was there from Michigan. He is very quiet, like Herbert Hoover."

"In that office Mr. Winkler sits in a glass cage all alone and two pretty girls sit outside. Mr. Cook is in a corner like at school."

"Business is beginning to look brighter in Valsetz. The water is getting higher in the reservoir. The road isn't so dusty. Four babies

41

were born, and the green bugs have stopped eating the sweet peas."

"Advertisement
Now I lay me down to slumber on the nicest smoothest pile of lumber.
I heard a voice - 'Hello, is this the Cobbs & Mitchell number?
Please send me a million feet of lumber. I slept all night. At nearly
dawn I awoke - the lumber pile was all gone."

"Mrs. Ann Heydon brought me a Dachshund dog from Michigan.
His name is Hitler and he is very meek."

"The Dallas baseball team beat the Valsetz team on the Valsetz
diamond a very small amount. We have a good team."

"The *Oregon Journal* was right. The mill pond did save Valsetz
from being burned. We hope they get the Pulitzer prize. They spoke
of getting it."

"One man told us that ten men were trapped in the blaze and that
we didn't have a chance. Another man told us some one was setting
fires on the railroad and on the county road and that we couldn't get
out. Mother put her hands over her ears—she can't stand much."

"Jingles: 'Bill Carver has been sitting there all day doing nothing
but wasting time.'
Kenny Goins: 'How do you know?'
Jingles: 'Because I have been sitting here watching him.'"

"Insurance man: 'You want your furniture insured against fire?'
Mrs. Denno: 'Yes, all except the clock. Everybody watches that.'"

JINGLES I
SUMMER-SEPTEMBER, 1938

Browsing through various issues of *The Star* I wondered what or who was "Jingles." No explanation nor identification—at first I thought it might be a mythical playmate of Dorothy's. My curiosity was aroused, yes stimulated sufficiently to initiate a thorough sleuthing. It certainly didn't sound foreboding. Jingles had a "happy face" sound to it.

I inquired of several people to no avail. Then in a meeting with Dorothy Anne's adult children, her son Fritz told me, "I think Jingles was a logger named Lambert. Don't know his first name or his whereabouts." The name Jingles didn't fit my mental image of a Valsetz logger.

A succession of phone calls ensued until I learned Jingles was Ingvar Lambert, living near Dallas, Oregon. His phone rang, answered by a deep, gruff voice. After identifying myself, I popped the question, "Are you Jingles?"

Ingvar chuckled and replied, "Yes." My search had ended.

My curiosity level whetted to the max, I asked the important question, "How did you acquire the name of Jingles?"

"Oh, I'm not going to tell you. I've told that story too many times."

For just a moment my heart fell down to my shoelaces. After all this sleuthing my curiosity wasn't going to be satisfied?" I began cajoling.

"Your nickname sounds interesting. People reading my book will want to know." I even made a formal plea, "Come on now, Mr. Lambert."

Success, he relented.

"Well, it seems I once told a joke around Valsetz about a Swede who hadn't been in America very long. You see, I'm a Swede, born in

Valsetz loggers standing atop one of the "small" logs taken out of Oregon's Siletz basin in the early days. Identified men, left to right, 3rd man, Woody Robinson; 4th, James Wasson; 6th, Eldon Keyes; 8th, Jingles Lambert; 9th, Norval Embree; 10th, Orville Robinson. (Photo courtesy Jingles Lambert)

Sweden."

"Ole was walking down the street in town one day when he suddenly spit a big stream of tobacco juice just as a well dressed lady walked by. Some of the brown goo splashed up on the lady's shoes.

She was horrified, began hollering for a policeman."

Ingvar was really getting into his story.

"Desperately looking for a place to hide, Ole ran into a hardware store. 'Can I hide in here from the policeman?' Ole asked the clerk.

'Sure,' he answered, 'jump into one of those sacks.'

Well, the cop arrived, asked the clerk, 'Did a Swede come running in here a few minutes ago?'

'Haven't seen anybody,' the clerk replied.

'What's in those sacks?' the cop asked, pointing his nightstick towards the sackful of Ole.

'Those are just chains we sell to loggers.'

The officer walked over to the first sack and gave it a kick with his scuffed brogue. As he did, the chains rattled proving the sack's contents. When he came to Ole's sack he gave it a hefty boot and from the sack came a man's voice, 'Yingle-yingle.'

And that's how I became known as Jingles, or if you prefer, Yingles," Ingvar concluded.

Dorothy Anne wrote about various Jingles happenings in several issues of *The Star*. She included a running narrative on a touching love story between Jingles and his wife Maxine that continues even today, fifty-eight years later. There will be more heart-moving Jingles experiences in the ensuing chapters.

*   *   *   *   *   *

Dorothy Anne's weather forecast in the September, 1938 edition of The Valsetz *Star*: "A little rain."

"We still stand for peace but there isn't any."

"Great Britain is getting alarmed. They are our cousins."

"Mr. Chamberlain flew in a fast plane and had tea with Mr. Hitler in his castle on a hilltop. After tea he flew back to England. He is our cousin, too."

(1938 was the year of a strike by the workers in Valsetz. Electricity was supplied to homes from the mill when it was running.)

"There is lots of trouble in the world but we can't hear any of it because none of our radios say anything on account of the men wanting ten cents more so our camp is dark and down and we have no electricity only coal-oil lamps like mother used to have years and years ago when she was ten."

"We had a letter from a group of young newspaper editors in the Philippine Islands who publish a paper called 'The Bugle'. They read about *The Star* in a Manila newspaper."

"Nellie Hendrickson, the Assistant Editor, returned from spending a summer at the beach. She has a lovely golden tan like Carole Lombard."

"I had to stay home most of the summer and practice the piano and get my teeth straightened, and now school has opened, and I have to study fractions."

"Life is a problem."

"Grandpa Hobson with mother and me dressed in our best clothes and went to the State Fair at Salem. Mother wore her blue suit which she got reduced, and I wore my blue velvet coat which used to be Mrs. Heydon's, but was made over to fit me by Mrs. Grout, who sews. Grandpa wore a heavy gold watch chain and carried a cane."

"Mrs. Ann Heydon our postmistress, came over the hill on horseback thirty years ago, and has been here ever since. She has no car, and there are no horses."

"Daddy sent his old grey felt hat to the cleaners. He said it would have to last until the Republicans were back in office."

"Two more babies were born."

"Cobbs & Mitchell lumber is still nice and smooth,—but we can't do anything about it."

"Mrs. D.A. Grout left real fast for Salem to have her appendix out."

"The Bridge Club opened, and the ladies all argue."

"Mr. Thomas has a dry battery radio that works. He took it out of a car in Salem."

"Professor: 'Robert Burns wrote, *To a Field Mouse.*'
"Donald Denno: 'Did he get an answer?'"

"Vote for Chas. Sprague in November for the next governor of Oregon. The Republicans will soon be back."

DOROTHY ANNE LOSES HER HELPER
AUTUMN-OCTOBER, 1938

Down through the years lumber production in Valsetz was curtailed due to multifarious and dissimilar happenings. Ofttimes it was either too hot or too cold—forest fire danger or deep winter snows kept loggers house-bound. But there were man-made closures, too; strikes for better wages or working conditions; regional or national economic slowdowns that created lagging lumber sales and slimmed-down timber prices.

No work meant no wages, so during a prolonged strike in the Fall of 1938, many Valsetz timber families left the little community to find work elsewhere. Some residents decided to "ride it out." The food on their table was produce from their garden, berries ripening on logged-off hillsides, Oregon fruits from a relative's orchard, deer and elk meat from nearby forests and fish from the plenteous stocks in Northwest waters. These steadfast souls literally lived off the land.

One casualty resulting from the 1938 timber strike was Dorothy Anne's right-hand helper. Nellie Hendrickson's family economically relocated during the work stoppage. Perhaps, attempting to diversify the *Star*'s editorial beliefs to a more masculine tenet, Dorothy Anne selected nine-year old Franklin Thomas as her new Assistant Editor. Or maybe he was just a cute kid who occasionally smiled at her.

Franklin was the son of Cobbs & Mitchell Superintendent, and Mrs. H.F. Thomas. In the *Star*'s October, 1938, issue Dorothy Anne commented on her new Assistant Editor:

* * * * * *

"Our Assistant Editor, Nellie Hendrickson has moved away from Valsetz. We decided to get a man in her place and his name is Franklin Thomas. He is nine-years old and was named after President Roosevelt."

"Franklin's daddy is a Republican and his mother a Democrat, so we can get both sides of everything."

"He believes in Chas. Sprague for our next governor of Oregon, and he believes in peace if you leave him alone, and he will take a sock at Hitler if he ever lands in this country."

"Franklin has many ideas on many subjects, but he said he would want his money every month. He stands for the same things the *Star* stands for."

The Valsetz Star proudly proclaimed it was one year old in October, 1938.

Dorothy Anne reported, "With the September issue of *The Star* there was no peace any place. In Europe they were quarreling and thinking of war, and there was a strike in Valsetz. Now everything is peaceful. Hitler got more land and everybody in Valsetz got five cents."

"Last Monday, October 10th the mill and logging whistles blew loud and long—the strike was over and people were smiling and speaking again, and getting their frigidaires and cars back, and now we can finish paying for our '*Book of Knowledge*,' and the barber can sell his honey and Fred Schaad can get his new teeth."

"We have a long list of lawyers on our subscription list, and they are all Republicans. But some of the Democrats are smart, too."

"Mrs. Roosevelt is doing her hair a new way and President Roosevelt is building a new house."

"Next month Franklin will write a terrible article on Hitler. Watch for it in the November issue of *The Star*."

"Mr. Glen Rice, of Kansas City, where are you? Please write to us. We are sorry we talked about you."

"ADV. I think that I shall never see
Lumber quite so smooth and free
From all the knot holes, pitch and things
That Cobbs & Mitchell lumber brings.
Any man can dream and slumber,
Only Cobbs & Mitchell can make such lumber."

"There was a birthday surprise on Mother over at the Thomas' house. She came with cold cream on her face on account of not knowing about the surprise. There was a cake with candles. She is the same age as Mr. Grout. His age is in the May issue of the *Star*." (March)

"Mr. Templeton hurried into Valsetz with two strange men, and hurried right out."

"Mr. Kackley got a deer and Mr. Grout got some ducks."

"The Valsetz high school football team lost to Perrydale forty-five or fifty to nothing."

"We had a lovely letter from a woman in South America."

VALLEY AND SILETZ BECOME VALSETZ
AUTUMN-NOVEMBER, 1938

The little isolated logging and lumber town site of Valsetz had the unique distinction of never having been a public municipality. The hamlet had always been privately owned—first in 1904 by the founders, Cobbs & Mitchell, then their lumber broker, Herbert Templeton, bought the entire layout in 1947. And finally, Boise-Cascade Corp. took over in 1959 and operated the timber business for 25-years. In 1984, Boise-Cascade bulldozed all the homes and mill buildings, burnt the debris, covered the mess with dirt and planted an appropriate grave marker of seedling Douglas firs atop the destroyed town. R.I.P.

The first buildings on the Valsetz site, after O.A. Fanno's early cabin, were sawmill structures erected in 1919-20.

Lumber for those first buildings came from Valsetz logs processed at the Cobbs & Mitchell sawmill in Hoskins. As construction got underway, a few workers began batching at the townsite. More men swelled the camp's throng when the sawmill saws began slicing into giant virgin logs in 1922, and by 1923 nearly 300 men had formed the nucleus of the fledgling logging community.

The two lumber tycoons, Jonathan Cobbs & William Mitchell, had wanted to name the town Cadillac, a namesake of their hometown in Cadillac, Michigan. They soon discovered there was already a Cadillac, Oregon, so that idea was quickly scuttled. That's when the two-part name was contrived—"Val" from "valley", "setz" from the Siletz River, and the compound word, "Valsetz" was born in the manger of the Oregon Coastal Cascades.

*　　*　　*　　*　　*　　*

Oregon Republicans, including Dorothy Anne, were jubilant.

She reported in the November, 1938 issue of *The Star*: "We are extra special glad and thankful this month on account of Mr. Sprague (Charles) being elected our next governor of Oregon."

"He (Governor Sprague) wrote us a nice letter some time ago, and we put it in a vault in the bank. Franklin and I celebrated his winning by taking ten cents each of *The Valsetz Star* money and buying an extra large ice-cream cone."

"Franklin won't write the terrible article about Hitler this month on account of it being Thanksgiving and we can't say anything mean about anybody. But we won't say anything nice either, because we don't like him on account of the thorn he got in his cheek from the roses, so he ordered all flowers stopped along the parade. If President Roosevelt got a thorn in his cheek he would just laugh. He'd not stop the bouquets."   "Grandpa Hobson, over in Salem, how did you like the election? We haven't seen him yet, but we bet he is smiling. He has been a Republican for eighty-nine years."

"We bow our heads this Thanksgiving time, and give thanks:
For Republicans getting back into office, and having their pictures in the paper again.
For all the kind people in the world.
For Cobbs & Mitchell's nice smooth lumber.
And for the strike being over so we can have turkey for Thanksgiving dinner, instead of the beef stew with carrots we had planned on if we hadn't been working."

"Mrs. Roosevelt said on her trip out west that there would be a woman president of the United States some day, and I think so too, but Franklin thinks a woman's place is in the home."

"Daddy doesn't have to send his old gray felt hat to the cleaners any more. The Republicans are coming into office and he can get a new one."

"Franklin said he would never marry Greta Garbo because her hair is too straight, and he doesn't like her heavy stockings with the ribs."

"Franklin doesn't like the new upsweep coiffures. He doesn't care for ears."

Dorothy Anne's father, Henry Hobson, was camp cook for Valsetz' Cobbs & Mitchell Lumber Co. Here he is talking with Stewart Holbrook who was a well-known Northwest author. He wrote more than thirty books, mostly on the outdoors, forests, rivers, and the logging industry. (Photo courtesy Graham family)

"Mrs. Ann Heydon made a business trip to Portland last week. She brought back her fur coat and four new dresses."

"They are beginning to quarrel over in Europe again. It is nice to live in Valsetz. Nobody quarrels since the strike."

"The bridge club met at Mrs. Fraser's. Mrs. West was high, and Mrs. Thomas was second. Mother was high once."

"Adv. Go to Mrs. Chas. Spray's Beauty Parlor for the new upsweep coiffure. It's sweeping the country."

"The school improvement club would like to call the soup kitchen something nicer. *The Star* thinks 'School Recreation Room' sounds dignified."

OREGON'S HERBERT HOOVER AUTUMN-DECEMBER, 1938

Oregon Republicans were pleased as punch when one of their own, a man raised in Oregon, Herbert Clark Hoover, was elected 31st president of the United States in 1928. Some of the punch took on a bitter taste, however, when the country's economic collapse of the early 1930's was nicknamed, the *"Hoover Depression."*

Herbert Hoover was born in Iowa in 1874 and orphaned when he was eleven years old. The pre-teen lad was subsequently hustled off to the Beaver State to live with an uncle in Newberg. Uncle John Minthorn moved to Salem in 1888 to become president of the *"Oregon Land Co."*

Young Herbert attended "Friends Pacific Academy," which later became "George Fox College." He became interested in mining and geology at an early age. Uncle John had done right well for himself in Salem so he agreed to send our later-to- be-president to college.

In 1891, Hoover left Oregon for a pre-college learning experience in Palo Alto, California. Later, at the age of sixteen, he was in the first "pioneer class" at *"Stanford University"*, graduating in May, 1895 with an A.B. in geology when he was only twenty years old. As many do, Hoover met his wife-to-be, Lou Henry, at college. They married and raised two sons.

Herbert Hoover took office as U.S. President in 1929, not a good year to become president of anything. He remained stead-fast in his economic philosophies even though the country nearly fell down around his ears by the end of his term in 1933. Herbert Hoover died in New York City in 1964, having dedicated most of his life to public service.

*   *   *   *   *   *

Although Herbert Hoover had lost much of his popularity after he left office, Republican-biased Dorothy Anne had this to report in the December, 1938 issue of *The Star*:

"An awfully nice thing happened to us. We heard from Mr. Herbert Hoover, who was once our United States President, and he is interested in *The Valsetz Star*. He sent us an autographed photograph of himself. Everybody says he likes children, and is very smart. We are proud and happy."

"Merry Christmas to All our Readers, and To All the World."

"Franklin can't write the terrible article about Hitler this month on account of it being the month of 'peace on earth, good will towards men,'— and women too."

"We think if Hitler would get married and have a little boy and a little girl, he would not be so cruel because he would have to read stories to them and buy them skates, and go down in the woods and get a tree to trim for Christmas. And come home with packages under his arm. We feel sorry for him this month, but next month we will be mad at him again."

"Franklin drew the Santa Claus at the top of the page. He is like Walt Disney."

"Mr. Winkler, in the Cobbs & Mitchell office, is worried about money but daddy says everybody is."

"Mr. Frank W. Trower, who is president of the *"Trower Lumber Company,"* in San Francisco, sent us a poem composed by Adeline Merriam Conner, the blind poet laureate of the lumber industry.

'I hope that every lumberman, wherever he may be,
Will see the golden star of hope, above his Christmas tree.
I hope the coming year will bring the boon his spirit craves,
And peace, goodwill and happiness make radiant his day.'"

"The West Coast Lumberman's Association" in Seattle and the *"Western Pine Association"* in Portland, both say, 'Do not call Douglas Fir Oregon Pine. Please get it right.' If they were in the fifth grade they would have to have it right."

"Up in Washington where my Grandmother Stafford lives they voted for all the Democrats. It's not quite such a good state as Oregon."

"Ann Heydon is very rushed in the post office now. She hardly has time to build all three of her fires. She has too many stoves."

"School is very interesting this year. Everybody in Valsetz is very busy and very happy. Fred Shaad got his new teeth. Franklin says he will never marry, and I don't think I will either."

"Adv. Don't forget Cobbs & Mitchell lumber when you build your house next month. Build a nice smooth little house with Cobbs & Mitchell lumber."

"Weather Forecast: A little snow perhaps."

FREDDY FIR?
WINTER-JANUARY, 1939

How did the Pacific Northwest's most prolific and highly valued, bread-and-butter lumber producing fir tree acquire the moniker, "Douglas fir?" Why not, "Freddy fir", "Frank fir" or even "Phyllis fir?" Was Douglas a logger, a timber baron, or some lumberman's brother-in-law?

Distant as it may seem, David Douglas (1798 - 1834) was a Scottish botanist whose name was ultimately tacked onto millions of Northwest firs in a huge forest exceeding 65,000 square miles abutting the moisture-laden Pacific Ocean.

Douglas was not the first explorer to plant his flag on the mossy butt-end of a stately fir tree. In fact, an English naturalist, Archibald Menzies, first spotted the famous fir on a trip to the new world in 1795. Although Menzies kidnapped a couple of green fir specimens from our NW forest and took them back to England, nobody thought he was very serious about creating a new source of two-by-fours. And besides, the name "Menzies fir" wouldn't have had the catchy sound that we later enjoyed with "Douglas fir." In fact, those who "talk timber" call it "Doug fir."

David Douglas was described by his peers as a self-educated botanist and duly designated as an official collector by the prestigious *"Horticultural Society of London."* He departed jolly old England on his second trip to the new world in July, 1824, arriving at the Columbia River April, 1825. An eight-month voyage could cause a person to lose sight of their original objective—but not this unabashed, determined Scotsman.

Arriving in Oregon, somewhat north of Valsetz, but south of Seattle, Douglas was wildly excited to discover the abundant varieties of botanical bracken in our Northwest forests. The same stuff Valsetz loggers called brush, or in the jungle-like coastal areas—thick brush.

Engineer and conductor, P.W. "Casey" Jones, pictured with "Chatterbox," one of three rail coaches which hauled freight and passengers between Valsetz and Independence, Oregon. (Photo courtesy Ingvar Jingles Lambert)

The wandering Scotsman discovered things he'd never seen before; densely-growing salal, native Northwest salmonberries, wild licorice and bear grass, incessant rainfall lasting for days, weeks, even months during winter. So overly enthusiastic was Douglas with his huge array of collected botanical treasures that he fell, severely injuring his knee as he packed the specimens for a slow boat ride back to England.

Undaunted by his painful knee wound, Douglas spent several more months in the verdant Pacific Northwest, gathering and classifying the plethora of flora and fauna. He was greeted by friendly coastal Indians who shared their food and lodgings with this funny little man from far across the great waters who curiously dug up their shrubbery.

In the *"Royal Society's"* catalog, Douglas is credited with fourteen papers and hundreds of newly discovered trees, shrubs and herbaceous plants he introduced from the new world. Thanks to his discovery the Douglas fir was officially designated Oregon's state tree in 1939.

In a strange accident, the exploring Scotsman was said to have fallen into a pit in Hawaii and was gored to death by a wild bull when he was only thirty-six years old. Douglas was thirty-six years old, not the bull, as Dorothy Anne would have reported. Certainly not a very fitting end for a man credited with discovering and naming our magnificent fir tree.

* * * * * *

And in Valsetz on the first of the New Year Dorothy Anne had this to report: "Happy New Year to Everybody! We couldn't say it any sooner because we don't publish our paper on the first of the month."

"This is an especially wonderful month.
Billy Miller's mother over in Dallas was a hundred years old on the first day of January, and Grandma and Grandpa Hobson, in Salem, will be married 64-years on the 25th day of this month. Mother went over to shake hands with Mrs. Miller and to ask her how she lived so long, and she said to live to be a hundred you had to look on the sunny side, but Grandma Hobson said to be married sixty-four years you had to look on both sides."

"We won't say anything about Hitler this month because we are tired of him."

"On the first day of next October Mrs. Ann Heydon and I will leave Portland on the Postmasters' Special for Washington, D.C., New York, Florida, and San Francisco, to attend the Postmasters' Convention in Washington, D.C. We think we will have enough money.

We will each have an evening dress, and we are invited to have luncheon with Mr. Frank Trower in San Francisco. We hope Mr. Templeton knows somebody in New York so we won't have to pay for our lunch."

"Valsetz town is hidden far up among the hills,
And when you drive the mountain,
You almost get the chills.
People try to find the town and sometimes get a scare,
But until you come upon it, you wouldn't know it's there."

"Franklin wears glasses now, and looks much more like an editor."

"ADV. Spring will soon be here so order Cobbs & Mitchell lumber early. You can use every piece of it. Remember, it's nice and smooth."

"The road is very good over the mountain now, lots of mud and humps but very good."

"Donald Denno has charge of the new oil station in front of Mr. Grout's store."

"We have a new teacher in the first grade, Miss Leyton, she is young and pretty, and can play the piano and dance."

"Some of the children in the fifth grade lost their umbrellas, and Mr. Neville Chamberlain lost his, too, over in Italy."

"At the Jackson Day dinner in Washington, D.C., they had to pay a hundred dollars for a plate of food. We only charge forty cents here."

"Three more babies were born."

Winter Wonderland
Winter–February, 1939

When it isn't raining during the winter along the Oregon coastal mountain range, in all likelihood it's snowing. Deep snows often closed down the Valsetz logging operations so it wasn't an oddity when *The Star* reported weather-related work stoppages in February, 1939.

It was quite unusual, however, to read young Dorothy Anne's mature appraisal of snow-caused work closures from her adult-like viewpoint. Quite out of character for a nine-year old, she expressed concern for the loggers being out of work and missing paychecks. No juvenile frivolity about throwing snow-balls, sledding, building snowpeople or wishing for an extended blanket of the white covering. In one edition she said: "We are thankful that it snowed in Seattle, but not in Valsetz."

But who can malign the romanticist who sees only beauty and a fantasy wonderland in gossamer flakes of falling snow? On the logged-off hillsides stubby hemlock stumps were transformed by Mother Nature into gingerbread cupcakes topped with an abundant glaze of snowy white frosting. Logs arriving at mill-site on railroad flatcars were similarly bedecked with a covering of the fluffy whiteness, sharply delineating the outline of those immense sticks from the forest. The top logs looked like they had been slathered with a lavish layer of whipped cream.

Dorothy and the town kids often plowed through tall snowdrifts, walking crunch by crunch, merrymaking their way to the snowy-roofed schoolhouse. Yardside shrubbery and smallish trees along the way had sacrificed their brightly-hued greens, reds, and browns to winter's sameness. With snowflakes clinging to every twig and stem, nature's camera only choreographed scenes of black and white.

Perhaps hardest hit of all by heavy snows were the animals, especially the small creatures and birds, my, how the birds suffered. Acrobatic mountain chickadees, sparrows, winter robins, even jays, both gray and blue were forced to work hard to earn a living. Tiny feet hippity-hopped winged critters across snow banks scurrying from bush to tall grasses in search of seeds deposited by benevolent winter winds. The dwarf-like feathered songsters twittered as they hungrily mingled and socialized on the frigid snow.

As the town's few cars in the late 1930's began to move about Valsetz following a snowfall, those vehicles not winter stored in Hoskins, the pristine wonderland turned slushy and dirty on unpaved streets. Sounds around town, mostly from mill activity became muted, softened by the acoustical layer of snow covering everything.

Perhaps like other pragmatic, no-nonsense Valsetz residents, Dorothy disregarded snow because she had become calloused by the hardships winter had often created—bring on the rain, the liquid wet stuff—at least the men could work in it.

*   *   *   *   *   *

In snowbound Valsetz, Editor Hobson had this to report: "Weather forecast, Spring weather soon."

"We are having some trouble this month to keep working. All the loggers have gone home. The snow has been very deep, and Mr. McLean, our logging superintendent, is very discouraged. He likes for things to run smoothly, but he says they never will."

"Everybody says we will have war and that Hitler will soon be over to get us. Franklin says he will throw away his glasses and fight. He just had the chicken-pox but is taking cod liver oil and will soon be strong again and ready to fight."

"If we had war Hitler couldn't get over the hill to get us because he would get stuck in the mud, and if he flies over Valsetz in an airplane Mr. Thomas, our superintendent, will hurry down to the mill and shut the lights off real fast."

"Abraham Lincoln had character. The *Portland Oregonian* says our country needs more character like Lincoln had and we think so too."

"Mrs. Roosevelt never gets tired and she can knit without even looking at the knitting. She sleeps in the summer but not in the winter. She does just the opposite from a bear."

A POEM
"Think not so much of worldly things, and more of being kind.
Like Lincoln, who lived long ago, whose kindly face was lined.
He was kind and true, and more like Christ
Than anyone we know.—Loved every man on this old earth,
Both friend and wicked foe."

"Many important people were born this month, Al Cottis, and Abraham Lincoln, and Jody Rhodes, and Mr. Starr, and Eldon Keys, and George Washington, and Hank."

"Advertisement: The snow will soon be gone and building will commence. Order COBBS & MITCHELL lumber now. Remember, it's nice and smooth and not a stick is wasted."

"Local News

Miss Virginia Leyton, our pretty new teacher, ate in the dining room with one hundred and sixty loggers. She was very calm."

JINGLES II
WINTER–MARCH, 1939

This is the second chapter in the ongoing saga about Ingvar, "Jingles", Lambert, who could easily have been the Paul Bunyan of Valsetz. Standing straight and tall in his size twelve caulks, a vertical six, two, and well over two hundred, he was, in my estimation, a logger's logger. Please, there were no lumberjacks around here. That descriptive word would incite a brawl on any caulk-chewed saloon floor in Northwest timber country.

Even today, at ninety, decked out in down-home denim stagged trousers held midwaist by dazzling red "*Stihl*" suspenders, Jingles personified those early day forest workers loosely termed "timber-beasts."

Forty-years out of Valsetz, Jing, (that's the term of endearment his wife, Maxine, uses) appears ready as ever to return to the lofty and unlogged. When asked about that possibility, he replied, "Well, maybe not, I don't even get up out of a chair as easily as I once did." My reply, "Well, Ingvar, I don't either but at ninety you've got twenty years on me, and I don't mean that I'm a hundred and ten."

When I first stepped into the Lambert's neat country farm home near Dallas, Oregon, I was greeted by the man of the woods and Maxine, his petite wife of fifty-eight years. I immediately noticed an aura between them seldom displayed by long-term married folks. It can best be described as loving glances, starry-eyed romantic looks typical of teen-agers in love, not glances between two grandparents. When Jingles spoke, she hung on his every word, listening and looking at him like he had just uttered ethereal proverbs and these two were on their first date. There was no mistaking the twinkle in Ingvar's longing look when he spoke softly to Maxine. It seemed to be a very special romance, ongoing since 1941.

Perhaps with a hint of humor and irony, Dorothy Anne best summed it up in the April, 1941 issue of *The Star*:

"Jingles will be married very soon. He is terribly in love with Maxine. He hurried to Portland to buy a ring and was going to pay a hundred dollars for it, but when he got there he was so thrilled and excited he paid two hundred dollars for it."

You'll read more about Jingles and Maxine Lambert in later chapters of this book.

*　*　*　*　*　*

The Valsetz Star had a special editor's note: "Spring is here and the birds are singing in the hills. The daffodils are up and people in Valsetz are raking their yards and planting their sweet peas. But when they read the papers and listen to the radio there is a worried look on faces on account of Hitler wanting more than his share, like some of the kids at school. Franklin says not to worry there will be no war on account of Hitler turning into a sissy. He sits and sips tea with the ladies."

"We think we are in the 'hall of fame,' but we aren't quite sure. The National Library of Amateur Journalism has requested a complete file of 'The Valsetz Star' to be placed in the Benjamin Franklin Memorial in Philadelphia, Pennsylvania. The file will be bound, and will rest there for two thousand years. Franklin says it's fame, all right."

"Mr. Charles A. Brand, member of the State Board of Higher Education, wrote words of encouragement to us. He had a dachshund dog once, and it was so long it was killed while crossing the railroad track."

"We wish to thank The *Oregon Journal* in Portland for writing so many nice things about 'The Star.' They don't seem to mind because we are Republicans."

"ADV. IT'S SPRING! Repair all the old buildings and build some new ones. Order Cobbs and Mitchell lumber right away."

"Franklin and I were invited to be guests at the State Legislature in Salem a few weeks ago by Mr. Dan Clark and some other Republicans, but we couldn't go on account of chicken-pox and fractions."

"Governor Sprague said, 'Don't shake your head, shake a leg.'"

"Ann B. Heydon left for Salem with Mr. Lawrence Kribble to get her toe fixed. It doesn't sound romantic, but it was."

"Hank, who brings in the wood for the loggers, left real fast for Texas on account of them finding Ethyl on his oil lands."

"The first airplane ever to land in Valsetz was piloted by Ralph Romaine, of Albany, from whom we had a nice letter.
He was forced down and was out of gas and almost landed on top of the dryshed. Mr. Thomas, our superintendent, shuddered on account of having so much trouble already."

"Everybody says the picture of the editor of 'The Valsetz Star' in 'The Oregon Journal' of March 12th looks like Mrs. Roosevelt. We are very proud because Mrs. Roosevelt has a lovely spirit and a beautiful character. People say beauty fades. It's like my blue dress."

"We had another fine long letter from Mr. Frank Trower in San Francisco. Mother said she would rather read his letters than to read most books."

DENUDING THE HILLS
SPRING–APRIL, 1939

During Dorothy Anne's newspaper days, the immediate hillsides overlooking Valsetz were mostly devoid of the gigantic conifers that had been sawn and axed by earlier log harvesters. Before the brush and second-growth took over logged hills, only weathered grey stumps stood as lifeless monuments to a grand and glorious forest cut and shipped off for constructing and abetting America's destiny of progress. Hillsides logged earlier were already green with the second crop of young trees. This emerald greenness gave promise of a future economic livelihood for the 1940's sons and daughters of Oregon's logger families.

We shouldn't sorrow the bleak hillsides of grey leavings from the aftermath of the timbermen's gleanings. Like fallow fields in farming's rotating cycles, the time of barrenness was fleeting, and though even briefly, had immediate virtues. In removing the sunshield ceiling of dense conifer crowns, timber cutters opened the soil which stimulated growth of understory plants and shrubbery to provide a vital food chain for a variety of forest animals. There soon grew abundant sun-enriched browse for elk and deer; cones and seeds for ground feeders; succulent berries for the two-legged and four-legged critters.

But the forests of the Northwest are forever regenerating—slowly evolving by nature alone, faster with man's assistance through tree-planting, seeding, growing new trees through new technology.

If the early Valsetz loggers returned today they would be amazed. Third-growth logging is highballing on hillsides they originally logged in the early 1900's. Some of the "third-time" areas already support substantial crops of new conifers. The tree farm concept—growing trees as a cash crop like bottomland farming—has spread throughout the Northwest since the inception of the idea during the early 1940's. Today, throughout timber country, tree farms are as common as corn in Kansas.

*　*　*　*　*　*

In Valsetz under the heading of Special Editor's Note, Dorothy Anne reported: "We are so thrilled we can hardly breathe. Mrs. Roosevelt who was flying to Seattle on account of the stork, wrote us a letter and said she was pleased with 'The Star.'"

"Germany swallowed Czechoslovakia, Italy swallowed Albania, and everybody in the United States is swallowing goldfish. It's terrible!"

"We think the next president of the United States will be a Republican. We won't send a copy of 'The Star' to the White House this month because we don't want to make them mad."

"Mr. Templeton, our publisher in Portland, called on us and wanted to know if we had received any renewals on 'Star' subscriptions. Will everybody think real hard and if you owe us any money, please send it to us."

"There is a complete file of 'The Valsetz Star' in the University of Oregon Library, and in the Library of the University of California."

"Mr. Frank Trower in San Francisco said there is a new book out about the logging woods called, 'Holy Old Mackinaw,' but was not a book for ladies to read. Mother sent for it right away."

"Below is a verse written by Adeline Merriam Conner, who is the blind poet laureate of the lumber industry.
'I wonder as the lumberman pursues his hustling way,
  Out selling shingles, boards and joists,
  How frequently he seems to see, as in a pleasant dream
  The happy homes he helps to rear, with rosy lights agleam.'

Isn't that lovely? It's much better than Mother's poems."

"FLASH! The Kansas Retail Lumbermen will hold a convention at Salina, Kansas on May 11th and 12th.

We are putting on another shift to get ready for their orders."

"ADV. There was once a couple who married,

By some Cobbs & Mitchell lumber they tarried.

'Oh my,' said the bride, 'I should like to reside in a house built of lumber so fine.'

'Don't worry my sweet,' said the groom to the bride,

Dorothy Anne and her Assistant Editor, Franklin Thomas, peeking around the corner of a Valsetz company-owned home. (Photo courtesy Graham family)

'I've been saving my money for you. I called Mr. Templeton today, and ordered a car full for two.'"

(Phone in your order today for Cobbs & Mitchell lumber.)

"Grandma Hobson, who is eighty-two came over the hills to Valsetz. She said she wanted to live long enough to see the Republicans back. She loves Herbert Hoover."

"They sent some sand from Florida to put in Governor Sprague's shoes. He said they should have sent the sand to put under his shoes to keep him from slipping. Franklin and I laughed. We will call on him in Salem soon."

"Mr. Herbert Hoover, our only living ex-president, has been fishing on the McKenzie River in Oregon.

With him was Mr. Ben Allen who is one of our subscribers."

"Mr. Lawrence Kribble, who never smiled before, is now smiling day and night. It's on account of Ann Heydon."

"Daddy and Hitler were both born in April.

Hitler celebrated for two days, but daddy couldn't celebrate on account of fishermen and the turbine.

"Mr. Grout had to sleep in the basement on account of so many fishermen upstairs." (The trout fishing season in Oregon opened in April and Valsetz Lake was a popular angling spot.)

"Mr. O'Brien is visiting over at the Thomas house. Dorothy Denno will soon graduate. Franklin doesn't care for spinach and Jingles bent the fender on his new car."

Logger Lingo
Spring–May, 1939

As with most occupational niches, early Northwest loggers invented a language totally unique unto themselves. A stranger might wonder if he heard something like, "The donkey puncher watched the faller on his springboard while he heard the whistle punk call for slack on the haulback after the chaser unhooked a turn at the landing and the bull bucker (not a cowboy) frowned in disgust."

Nearly every logger and most woods jobs carried a unique moniker totally different from anything else in the civilized world. For instance, the "bull bucker" was the gnarly, tough as nails (usually), boss of all the cutting crew. The "donkey puncher" operated the steam donkey engine's drums and reels that collected logs to a central location, pulled in by a heavy stranded cable. The whistle punk, since replaced by electronics, stood where he could watch the rigging slingers and with a wire to the donkey engine signalled the necessary actions to haul in a turn of (several) logs to the landing (central point).

A "powder monkey" was a person who inserted a blasting cap and fuse (before electronics) into a single stick of dynamite (the primer) which would in turn be placed with more dynamite sticks and put beneath (hopefully) the object to be blasted, (usually a rock or stump, not the bull bucker's car).

The "buckers" usually worked independently sawing downed trees, pulling a misery whip, before chainsaws came to the woods. The trees were cut into pre-determined lengths, usually 24, 32 or 40-feet long for ease in truck hauling. They bucked up trees felled by other loggers or storm-related blow-downs.

The biggest danger for buckers was the potential for log sections to roll over them as occasionally they had to work below the log being sawed. Bridged trees would often bind bucker's saws, creating frustrations and perhaps a few choice examples of "logger lingo." Buckers usually sawed downward but sometimes a bridged tree would cause them to change tactics and saw upwards to avoid a bind.

All early buckers and fallers depended on their manual saws to get the job done. In some outfits, bucking and falling was contracted on a piece basis. This was termed "busheling" and their earnings depended on their production. But the best friend to the cutters was the camp's saw filer. Saws were usually brought in daily and exchanged for a sharp one. The saw filer was a professional, knew exactly how each man preferred the "set" of his saw and the length of the "rakes" of the teeth, as well as being sharp enough to cleanly snip a wisp of hair from a barroom gal's lovely head.

The long "misery whips" were handled carefully by all concerned.

Buckers and fallers were responsible for carrying the saws to and from the cutting site. They carried the long bands of razor sharp steel balanced very carefully on their brawny shoulders, teeth edge out, please! Taking a tumble into the salal with a saw was bad enough but could be extremely hazardous to their health if the knife-like teeth were pointed inwards at the man's jugular.

*   *   *   *   *   *

In *The Valsetz Star* Dorothy Anne admitted she had made a terrible mistake that was caught by Mr. Girard, editorial writer for the *Philadelphia Inquirer*. "He reminded me I said Grandpa Hobson had been a Republican for eighty-nine years which was impossible because that was four years longer than the Republican party had lived. But we bet Grandpa was thinking about the Republicans those first four years!"

"We have been reading the Postmasters' Gazette, and some wonderful things will happen at the Convention in Washington, D.C. next October 9th. President Franklin D. Roosevelt will make the principal address and Mrs. Heydon and I will attend a reception at the White House for the ladies, where they will be received by Mrs. Roosevelt. We will stay at the Mayflower Hotel which will be official headquarters for the convention. It's very expensive. When our money is gone we will hurry to Florida where Mrs. Heydon's sister lives, and it won't cost us anything."

"Mr. Chas. F. Jenkens, of Philadelphia, a friend of ours through *The Star*, has sixty different kinds of hemlock trees growing on his Germantown estate. It is the world's biggest show of the hemlock family. Mr. Jenkens also believes in Republicans and Kindness, like *The Star*."

"The King and Queen of England brought two hundred and ninety-five suitcases with them on their trip to Canada and America. When Mrs. Heydon and I board the Postmaster's Special we will have only two."

"Mrs. Franklin Roosevelt has nine new costumes which she will wear when the King and Queen arrive, but she will not wear them all at once."

"At the state dinner in Washington when President and Mrs. Roosevelt entertain the King and Queen of England, they will have calves head soup, beets and sweet potatoes, and flounders, and ice cream, same as us."

"We have a dog, his name is Reno—he is very active."

"Mrs. Ann Heydon received a beautiful post office diploma from President Roosevelt and she was confirmed by Senator McNary, and she has James Farley's picture on her radio, and she gathers rhododendrons with Lawrence Kribble."

"In our Junior Weekly Reader it says that China had opened her back door."

"Princess Elizabeth, of England, who is heir to the British throne, just celebrated her thirteenth birthday, and received her first pair of long silk stockings. But Betty Blazer, in our grade, has been wearing them for a long time."

"Franklin spent several days in Portland. Mr. Leslie Street, our good kind timekeeper, is leaving Valsetz. He will work in Salem. We are sorry. Mr. Richard Ardelle, who sounds like the movies, will take his place.

Jingles takes Miss Leyton the pretty teacher, for rides."

ELUSIVE BLACKBERRIES
SPRING–JUNE, 1939

And oh, those berries! The tiny elusive, wild mountain blackberries that Dorothy Anne and her schoolmates picked on logged-off Valsetz hillsides were prized as though they were gold-plated. Not a pie has ever been baked to rival the mountain blackberry. It's distant cousins, the Northwest's Evergreen and Himalaya, make splendid jelly, wine, and bird food, but the large seeds fail to satisfy a gourmet blackberry-lover's taste buds.

Northwesterners guard the location of their favorite mountain blackberry patch like buried treasure. Neighbors have been known to arise before dawn to follow knowledgeable pickers to their secret berry patch locations, usually in logged-off areas. Bucketsful of the shiny black delicacies bring top dollar for entrepreneurial pickers. Gathering the berries has become a learned NW skill. It would seem the wily little buggers instinctively grow in a manner to deceive pickers. The berries are found under leaves and branches; hidden behind stumps; growing in dense grass and ferns. At first glance you'll see nothing. Push aside foliage and—voila—there's where the little black buttons are hiding.

Another unique NW berry, although not prized like the above, is the yellow/red salmonberry. Kids relish eating the cap-shaped fruit right off the bushes during early summer. Valsetz youngsters found them in abundance along low-lying, marshy streams. Unlike blackberries, the salmonberry bushes, growing to heights of 8 - 10-feet, prefer shadier locations with minimal sun but abundant moisture.

Coastal people ate both salmonberry sprouts (tender shoots) and the berries. They peeled the sprouts and ate them raw, as do many

Northwest youngsters. They could also be steamed and eaten like asparagus (the sprouts, not the youngsters.) While blackberries lend themselves to drying, salmonberries contain too much Northwest H-2-O and about the time they are dry, only seeds remain. Thimbleberries, black raspberries, (blackcaps), and huckleberries round out the list of delicious NW berries found in the wild.

In Dorothy Anne's childhood the great outdoors surrounding Valsetz became the youngster's playground. They got along fine without T-V in the early days because they didn't miss what they never had. Picking berries provided income and delicious edibles while teaching early work habits and responsibilities.

*   *   *   *   *   *

In the June, 1939 edition of *The Star*, Dorothy Anne proudly announced: "This issue of '*The Star*' is dedicated to the Oregon Newspaper Publisher's convention, to be held at Timberline Lodge June 28-30.

Franklin and I were invited to be their luncheon guests on Friday but we cannot be there on account of having nobody to leave in our office. Every time the door is left open our papers blow all over everything. It's awful.

As soon as our paper gets a little bigger we will pay somebody to stand at the door."

"We have subscribers all over the United States; three in Canada, two in the Hawaiian Islands, one in Cuba, and three in South America."

"When the King and Queen arrived in Washington, D.C., it was thrilling. Everybody shook, but nobody dipped. President Roosevelt placed his top hat over his heart, and Mrs. Roosevelt got ready for dinner in fifteen minutes."

"Following is a poem entitled 'About Editors,' written
by Adeline Merriam Conner:
'I wonder about editors, and how on earth they keep their poise
Amid strange inadvertencies which mar their days with strife and
noise;—Our editors are proper folk, who seldom rave and tear their
hair, But still I wonder how they stand, the everlasting wear and
tear.'"

"When we leave on the postmaster's special, Mrs. Heydon will
wear her traveling tweeds and I will wear my traveling twill. We will
gaze at the Statue of Liberty in New York, and see the Empire Building, and Coney Island, and Kate Smith."

"ADV. Just dial our number, and order some lumber,
It's the best that money can buy. Order from Cobbs & Mitchell
now, because it's really not very high."

"On Friday evening, June 2nd, Valsetz had the first formal dance
it ever had in its life. Everybody was excited. Mrs. Grout and Mother
hurried to Portland and had their faces lifted, but it didn't last—fell
the night before the dance. There was bare shoulders and gold slip-
pers and high hair, and low hair, and gardenias and perfume, and
gum. It was swell!"

"Mother borrowed a dress and bought some flowers and borrowed
a man, on account of daddy not dancing. He is a Republican, not very
gay, but very sensible.
Mr. Thomas wore tucks, and Dick Arnelle couldn't wear his on
account of a boil."

"Mrs. Heydon wore the largest red flower in the world. Heels and toes and backs were out. Nobody ever saw anything like it."

"Dorothy Denno looked beautiful when she graduated. She wore long flowing white, and is slim and dark like a wood nymph. Mrs. Denno cried. It was sad."

"School is out, our teachers have gone. We had a last day picnic, and all said goodbye."

"The Valsetz baseball team is the best team in the world. They win every game. Next year they will play the New York Giants."

"Mr. C.L. Starr, our Vice-President, came from Portland and spoke to the high school graduating class."

VALSETZ FIRE
SUMMER–JULY, 1939

In the July, 1939 issue of *The Valsetz Star*, Dorothy Anne mentions a ravaging fire that destroyed portions of the town.

"Everybody was excited. Mrs. Heydon lost her post office and her apartment with the pretty bathroom. She ran downstairs in bare feet with housecoat flying open. Someone ran up to her apartment and saved a ball of twine, a half- bottle of mucilage, an empty perfume bottle, a picture of George Washington and an evening dress."

Donald Denno, who arrived in Valsetz in 1922 when he was two-years old, recalls that fire.
"As I remember it, the fire was started by a young boy playing with

matches," he said. "The blaze destroyed much of the town's business section. For awhile, the residents feared it could race out of control and spread to more buildings. Luckily, the wind changed and volunteers were able to bring the fire under control. But, for awhile it was frightening."

Down through the years fire played a major role in the destiny of the little logging community. Originally, Valsetz came into existence as the aftermath of a devastating regional forest fire in 1910. Several ensuing forest fires threatened the community in subsequent years, but the town managed to survive. Various blazes within the town's perameter damaged sections in later years, but the townsfolks and the owners were able to hang on.

The final blow, Boise-Cascade's economic decision to close the mill in 1984, brought Valsetz' seventy-five year existence to a close. This time the mill, the homes, bunkhouses and stores did not escape the flames which purposely consumed the town by corporate decree, and wiped it off the face of Oregon's map.

* * * * * *

In the July, 1939 issue of *The Star*, Dorothy Anne reported, "We are late with our edition this month on account of our visit up in Washington with my Grandmother Stafford who is a Republican, and our business district burning, and the terrible heat, and having to pick wild blackberries to pay for Mrs. Heydon's expensive blue shoes which she lost in the fire."

"Franklin Thomas, the Assistant Editor was very heroic during the fire. With his sister, Marjorie Jean, and the Scully twins from Portland, he climbed to the top of the building twice through smoke and carried things out."

"The mill was saved again, because the wind went straight up instead of across."

"Now Mrs. Heydon has to take a bath in a bunkhouse in a tin wash tub."

(It must have been very disappointing for Dorothy Anne to report this item:) "We have to give up our trip to the Postmaster's Convention in Washington, D.C. in October. We are sorry we will not be able to shake hands with President and Mrs. Roosevelt at the convention, but Daddy says never mind—just wait a little while and we can go to Washington, D.C. and shake hands with some Republicans."

"We play all day in our sun suits. Hitler seems far away and not very interesting, and we don't seem to care what the Roosevelts do."

"Daddy hasn't had his vacation yet. He doesn't know whether to go to Breitenbush to reduce, and gain again like last year, or to go to Crawfordsville and meet some of the daughters of the girls he used to know."

"Mr. James Farley says the next president of the United States will be a Democrat, and *The Valsetz Star* says the next president will be a Republican. We are a member of the Marion County Young Republican Club."

"Mr. Palmer Hoyt, Publisher of 'The *Portland Oregonian*,' says women rule the world."

"ADV. Lumber ships sail o'er the ocean,
At every port they dock
Leaving Cobbs & Mitchell lumber
To make floors for queens to walk."

"When the fire raged in the business district last Sunday, we packed up our 'Book of Knowledge' again—second time-and Daddy's law books but he isn't a lawyer, and 'The History of The Republican Party,' and, 'How to be Happy Though Married,' which is Mother's book."

"Mrs. Heydon's four guns were burned in the fire, and Doctor Spray lost all his cod liver oil and pink cold tablets. Only one life was lost. Mr. Grout's mouse cat was locked in the warehouse which burned."

"Daddy says if Hitler and Mussolini would come over to this country and eat hot dogs with mustard we would not have any war."

"Mother only looks forty-nine when she is dressed up."

"Valsetz is small but very exciting. One couple got married, one couple got divorced, three men got in a fight, two babies were born and two men got in jail."

"Greta Garbo can milk a cow."

"Franklin and I say our prayers every night."

"When Grandpa Hobson gave up his job at eighty-four years of age, it took two men to take his place. He is a Republican."

Timber Jobs
Summer–August, 1939

In the early days around the Northwest, logging became a learned skill usually passed down from family elders to their youngsters.

There were many different logging tasks, each requiring varied knowledge and experience. Some jobs were mundane and could be learned after brief instruction. The younger entrants to the logging job market often started as skid road greasers, gathering firewood for donkey boilers, setting chokers, or bull-cook helpers around the messhall and bunkhouses.

The more advanced work functions such as falling, high-climbing, donkey punching, whistle punk, loading, train engineer and switch-man, or powder monkey required training or experience. In some highball operations safety and maturity was sometimes forsaken for expediency, often with disastrous results.

Before power chainsaws, eight and ten-foot long steel, two-man, misery whip saws were the tools of choice for the breed of logger trained as a faller. It was their responsibility to cut down the tree, often six to ten-feet in diameter, fall it exactly where it would be easiest to buck into sections and haul away, while minimizing damage to the tree or others in the area. In competition, experienced fallers could hit a stake and drive it into the ground with the tree they were falling, regular sharpshooters.

During the onset of logging, when timbermen thought the virgin forests were inexhaustible, fallers often left five to ten-foot tall stumps, avoiding pitch and swelled butts near the tree's root system. But times are a'changin'. Today's fallers leave low stumps, harvesting all the wood they can get—pitch and swelled butts be damned. With short supply, wood is money in the bank.

Fallers worked in pairs standing on springboards jammed into chopped notches in the tree. A springboard was a six-foot length of straight-grain fir or spruce, six or eight-inches wide and capped at the tree-end with a metal shoe or plate which would "bite" into the notch. It became a platform for the faller to stand on whilst he chopped and sawed.

Notch-height determined how much stump was to be left, the springboard notch was cut five to ten feet above the ground. A pair of "matched" fallers usually meant one man could chop right-handed, while the other was left-handed, for chopping out the undercut which determined the tree's direction of fall.

The pair of fallers carried their springboards into the woods along with double-bitted axes, saws, oil bottles for lubricating the saw, wedges, mall and their "feedbag" or lunch pail. On large trees two or more springboards were needed as the fallers worked their way around the monster.

When the final sawcut had been made approaching the upper slant of the undercut and the noble conifer began to topple, the fallers would jump off their springboards yelling the proverbial, "timber," to warn anyone nearby to skedaddle.

The fallers avoided jumping straight back from the tree to eliminate potential injury from the tree trunk's "kickback," as it fell. As with most logging, falling was dangerous work with men exposed to descending limb "widow-makers," and the tree "kickback." With many safety precautions and stringent OSHA regulations, today's logging environment, while still dangerous, is a much safer place to work than during early Valsetz days.

*　*　*　*　*　*

In August, 1939, another dignitary recognized *The Star* and Dorothy Anne. She reported: "The nicest thing that happened to us this month was our letter from Oregon Senator Chas. L. McNary, who is a very important Republican in the United States Senate. He wrote such big words, but they sound important.

Senator McNary isn't tired of life, but he is tired of politics, and wrote for us to come on out and see his farm near Salem with the orchards and flowers and vegetable gardens, and Charlotte's pony, Dandy, and he is sure we will think him a better farmer than legislator."

"Gleiwitz, Germany is bristling, Senator Claude Pepper of Florida shook his fist at Congress, Hitler stunned everybody and corsets are coming back."

"Franklin and I hope that President Roosevelt won't change the Christmas tree." (After FDR arbitrarily moved Thanksgiving.)

"ADV. Just hear the rustle, the noise and the bustle,
As the orders swing into line.
It's C & M lumber, as smooth as a bumber,
Just order it any old time.
P.S. 'Bumber' isn't in the dictionary, but it rhymes."

"Last year Mother planted a package of perennial flower seeds. Only one seed came up. In the winter she covered it with a little roof, and when it got real cold she put straw over it and two warm stones close by at night.

Yesterday it bloomed. It was a weed!"

"When Andrew Carnegie was asked which he considered the most important factor in industry—Labor, Capital or Brains, he replied, "Which is the most imporant leg of a three-legged stool?"

"Mr. Paul McNutt and Daddy are both quite handsome but Daddy's stomach is too big for a sunsuit."

"Professor Ernest Albert Hooton, of Harvard, said if marriages were made in the Ford factory instead of in heaven, they would last longer."

"*The Valsetz Star* is still only 2 cents per copy, or $1.00 per year by mail."

"The Bridge Club got so hot they meet at night."

"Lee Fallin, crack pitcher for the Valsetz baseball team, was seen giving an ice cream cone to Virginia Powell."

"Mr. Lawrence Kribble is making Mrs. Ann Heydon a new set of furniture out of Cobbs & Mitchell's nice smooth lumber."

"Fashion note: Ladies will wear bustles in the back and ostriches on their heads."

"The Republicans are very sensible, but the Democrats are lots of fun. Sometimes we don't know what to do."

"The new Cobbs & Mitchell store, managed by Mr. Grout, has a new walk-in ice box, and looks like Seattle."

"Leonard Younce: 'I wonder why there are so many more automobile wrecks than railroad accidents?'
Dave Dixon: 'That's easy. Did you ever hear of an engineer hugging the fireman?'"

Donald Denno
Summer–September, 1939

Donald Denno of Salem, arrived in Valsetz with his parents in 1922 when he was two-years old. He and his sister, Dorothy, attended school in Valsetz, graduating in 1939 when there were only six other seniors in the graduating class.

"My sister was a year-and-a-half younger than I was and made it through high school in three years," Denno recalled. "She was very ambitious, wanted out of Valsetz and was anxious to get on with her life. Following high school, Dorothy attended business college. Later, after the war began, she joined the women's navy, in those days called the WAVES."

With a complacent gaze into the past, Denno reminisced, "We lived comfortably in Valsetz, always had plenty of food on the table. I don't really remember any severe hardships." Then with an impartial smile, he said, "Of course, I'd lived there through all my growing up years, didn't really know anything different."

Prior to the Depression, the Denno family lived at Cobbs & Mitchell's old camp six, located a couple of miles up the tracks from Valsetz. "Cobbs & Mitchell closed down for awhile during the Depression and we moved into one of the company-owned homes in Valsetz where we toughed it out during the hard times," Denno recalled. "During my dad's career in Valsetz, he worked as a brakeman on the railroad and also as a timekeeper."

During the late 1930's the Denno family lived next door to the Harry Starr family in a comfortable company-owned house. Starr was the planing mill superintendent. Denno reiminsced, "I worked in the planing mill trying to put money aside for college, and I was glad to have the job."

"I recall we had a cozy home with a wood burning stove that had coils for heating water. We burnt planer ends from the mill which were always available for Valsetz homes."

"I'd saved enough to start school at the University of Oregon in 1939," Denno recalled. "During the summers I'd go back to Valsetz and work for Cobbs & Mitchell, usually in the planing mill."

"When jobs were hard to find I even washed dishes for Dorothy Anne's dad, Henry, in the company kitchen. He'd tell me, 'You'll make it big someday like Wendell Willkie.' He was the Republican presidential candidate in 1940 and I guess he had washed dishes for a living in his younger days. I can remember Dorothy Anne's newspaper. I would often fold the papers for her prior to mailing."

Denno continued, "Another part-time job I had was renting boats on Valsetz Lake, the company's millpond. We had excellent trout fishing there." With a chuckle, Denno said, "One day while fishing with Frank Heydon we looked across the lake and saw Bert Babb and Bert Thomas standing waist-deep in water. They had swamped their canoe and had scrambled over to a half-submerged log. Bert Babb yelled at us, 'Get a boat over here, take your time but hurry up.'"

On another subject, Denno reminisced, "There was a dairy ranch near Valsetz that used to deliver milk in town. When it went out of business the owners rounded up all but two or three cows they couldn't catch. The dairyman was reimbursed for the renegades and when fresh meat became scarce, one of the Valsetz men went, 'cow hunting,' and we had beef on the table for quite awhile."

World War II interrupted Denno's college education but he was discharged in 1945 and resumed school at U. of O.

Denno retired from Sears-Roebuck in 1980 as a hardware buyer in Chicago, after putting in 33-years with the retail giant.

The retired buyer was nonchalant when describing his childhood years in Valsetz. "There were a few lean years but people in those days learned how to get by with less. We were more pragmatic and depended on each other more so than today.

If you had two loaves and your neighbor had none, you shared and both of you made it through with one loaf."

"The good old days?" I asked facetiously.

"Yes, I suppose so," Denno replied with a smile.

*　*　*　*　*　*

Talk of war had even spread to Valsetz as Dorothy Anne reported in *The Star*'s September, 1939 issue:

"Everybody in Valsetz talks about war all the time, and the radio talks about war and the papers talk about war. We wish we could talk about something else, but nobody listens."

"Besides we couldn't go to war anyway because Franklin's legs are too thin and the editor is the wrong sex, so if our readers don't mind we will try to write poetry and talk about peaceful things like Daddy thinking he can go to war again and for two weeks he didn't eat any bread or potatoes, and his stomach is the same size as ever."

"Over in Europe they are cracking and shooting and smashing, and over in America we are going back to school Monday."

"We will keep the American flag waving at the top of 'The Star' until there is no more war in the world."

"Daddy said let Hitler take his tricks first, because like in bridge, it wasn't always so hot at the last."

"Everything over in Europe is all mixed up, and Walter Winchell (radio newscaster) wants peace, and Mr. Ickes has a new baby, and Valsetz will be neutral."

"We hope that peace will come again, war will go away.
We think that God can help us out, if we will only pray."

"In the last issue of '*Hoo Hooter*,' a lumbermen's magazine, there is a picture of Frank W. Trower, president of the '*Trower Lumber Company*,' in San Francisco, who has written many fine letters to '*The Star*.' We thought he was elderly but in his picture he is quite young and handsome."

"Mrs. Wisecarver, postmaster of McMinnville, will be one of the Oregon ladies to stand beside Mrs. Roosevelt at the convention tea for ladies in October."

"Mrs. Heydon will have her tea in her bunkhouse, and the editor will have milk in the cookhouse instead of at the Mayflower Hotel in Washington, D.C. as we had planned."

"ADV. And when you live in a house built of Cobbs & Mitchell's nice smooth strong lumber - no bombs can get you."

"Valsetz is quiet this month.
Alex Mitchell and Evelyn Turner got married, and Eldon Keyes can't find his wife."

"Everybody is complaining about their foundations. Cliff hasn't the time to fix them."

"Mrs. Grout and Mother haven't washed their faces since the beauty shop lady in Portland told them not to in June. Franklin and I have to wash our faces three times a day."

"Dorothy Denno left to attend business college in Portland.

Marjorie Jean Thomas for her senior year at Holy Child Academy, and Dale Appleton and Donald Denno for the University of Oregon."

"Jingles had his tonsils out."

"Mother has some new corsets for a waist like a wasp, but when she laces them real tight she faints."

Mr. W. T. O'Brien, of Portland, who is Franklin's grand-father, was visiting over at the Thomas house. He dressed up in his white linen suit and sat in the grandstand, watched the Valsetz Baseball Team beat the Portland Babes."

WOOD WORMS REVOLUTIONIZE LOGGING
AUTUMN–OCTOBER, 1939

Like no other invention, with the possible exception of snoose, the chain saw changed the way we cut wood and revolutionized the lumber industry.

From the time man toppled the first tree and then realized it could be sliced up into boards, timber cutting had been done with brute strength—muscle-power applied to handsaw, axe or early man's stone adze.

Surprisingly, the idea of a power chain saw harks all the way back to the mid-1850's when some enterprising, and probably strained muscle individual, applied with the U.S. patent office to license the idea. He undoubtedly conjured up the vision of building megalopolis-size cities from planks he'd carved from tree-trunks with a putt-putt saw.

But, there were multitudinous obstacles—not the least of which was the cutting device. Would it be chain, cable, gear, knife or saw blade? Nobody had the foggiest idea. But at least the entrepreneurs headed in the right direction trying to devise a linked cable or guided chain as the cutter.

A patent was issued for a prototype chain saw in England around 1900. Sorry, you loggers, the darned thing didn't work very well.

Stihl, inventors kept trying. Get the hint? In 1925, German engineer, Andreas Stihl, manufactured the *first* "portable" chain saw. Well, it was kind of portable. Without industrial insurance in those days, loggers feared repetitive hernias from lugging around the German saw. It weighed 140-pounds. It seemed that excess weight was one of the prototype's early curses.

German Andy sold a few of his monsters in Europe but they flopped like Y2K insurance policies in North America. A few years later a Portland, Oregon, company developed three different models weighing in at around 70 - 90 pounds. Still (I won't use it again), tree-wise Northwest loggers wouldn't go for them.

They said the cutting action left a lot to be desired.

Finally, yes, at last, Andy's engineers devised a near-acceptable model. It weighed around forty-five pounds. Cutting action? Not real good but somewhat better than a stone adze.

Stihl salespeople caught the next boat to America and presented the improved saw to the U.S. timber-cutters. They turned thumbs down. Wait a minute, now what was the problem? It was a German saw and Germany's Hitler was beginning to blitzkrieg Europe. No Sale!!

Some wise old graybeards deduced that loggers, like the rest of us, resisted change and feared new-fangled things that were cantankerous and emitted nasty smoke and fumes. Mr. *Stihl* sold some of his saws in Canada but U.S. loggers shied away from the contraption. Then along came WWII and we all had more problems than chain saws.

The balance of this tale sounds like a logger's tall story told around the bunkhouse barrel-stove late in the evening, but never-the-less is true.

A young upstart named Joe Cox was working in the piney woods of Eastern Oregon after the war. He'd seen a few clattering, unpopular rattle-trap saws and recognized the major obstacle seemed to be the cutting action.

One day, while sweating down an unusually stubborn pine, Cox observed a fallen, bug-infested log. Upon closer examination he noticed wood worms tunneling their way through the tree trunk, zipping along quick as a politician's promise. He wondered how they could chomp through the wood so lickety-split.

The next day, the young logger, recently migrated from Oklahoma, brought a powerful magnifying glass to the the buggy log. He laid down beside it, fascinated by the up-close view of the wood worms' choppers. Undaunted when his fellow loggers threatened to call in the men in the white coats with their butterfly nets, he learned how the worms cut their tunnels. Their cutting action seemed to be a side-to-side motion rather than straight forward burrowing.

Cox began duplicating the worm's choppers in the basement of his Portland home. The young engineer perfected the chain and the bar-guide through continuous trial and error. While Cox was inventing the first successful chain, "*McCullough*" developed the first light-weight engine, and the rest, as they say when the water goes over the dam, is history. We understand *Stihl* also improved on their earlier models.

And that's the story of a self-made multi-millionaire who became fed-up with hand-sawing trees so invented a better mousetrap.

* * * * * *

"This month in Valsetz everybody is eating pumpkin pie, and the maple leaves are falling, and Eddie Cantor had a boy, and Hank had a birthday, and Columbus discovered America and the wild geese are all going south," reported Dorothy Anne.

"We wish our subscribers could read some of the nice letters we receive.

There is a little old man, eighty-five, in Boston, Mass. who reads *The Star* for breakfast when it comes. He hasn't much money.

A woman at the Old Folks Home in Philadelphia, who wrote that she loves God and *The Valsetz Star*.

A man in Denver, Colorado, who sells shoestrings would like to subscribe to *The Star*, but he hasn't any money. We sent him a whole file of them.

And then the airline stewardess in Salt Lake City, who said she read *The Star* as she flew thru the clouds.

The big, fat, gay, rich lumberman from Michigan who renewed his subscription and sent twice too much money. We didn't send any back.

A manufacturer from St. Louis, who said the Republicans were sane and safe and sensible and rock-ribbed.

A railroad conductor in Chicago, a good Democrat, said that we take our politics too seriously. But Daddy said somebody had to be serious.

And there is Mr. Case, a Seattle insurance man, who had a terrible thing happen to his rock-ribbed Republican uncle in Marion, Kansas.

He raised a son and two daughters to be Republicans. All three of them married Democrats and the two daughters turned into Democrats as soon as they married, and the son's wife wouldn't turn into a Republican so he only got one Republican out of the six. It was a terrible mess!"

Our publisher, Mr. Herbert Templeton, in Portland, has a new granddaughter born in Herkimer, New York, October 3rd. Her name is Camilla Cristman,"

"Benjamin Franklin said in 1773, 'There never was a good war or a bad peace.'"

"Mrs. Roosevelt said she wouldn't have a wasp waist. Mother has given it up, too."

"Franklin and I would like to say thru the press that we are not babies any more, and that we are tired of spinach and carrots and cereal. We would like to have pie three times a day. We hope our Mothers will read this."

"Ann B. Heydon has moved into her new post office in the old depot. She has a bay window. All her life she has wanted a bay window."

"Mother paid ten dollars for her new 'wasp' corset, but she doesn't want anybody to know it."

"Mr. and Mrs. Grout celebrated their silver wedding anniversary on the ninth of October. All their friends came and gave them a sterling silver vegetable dish.
    Their candles were silver, and the cake was silver, and they won the silver money, and they both have silver hair."

"Franklin has a new girl friend. She is twenty-two."

"Eldon Keyes found his wife."

"There is a new boy in school who can box and ride horses and play tennis and dance and can swear in four languages."

"ADV. 'Phone your orders right away, cause we're shipping night and day. Cobbs & Mitchell nice smooth lumber."

LOG HARVESTING GOES HIGH-TECH
NOVEMBER, 1939

Lumber production in the United States seemed to hit its peak in 1925 when more than forty-billion board feet rolled off sawmill green chains. In just five years, (1930) the total output had fallen to slightly over twenty-six billion feet, then hit bottom during the 1932 Depression at ten-billion, as many mills closed or cutback drastically. The Valsetz production seemed to approximate the national trend although the mill had been operating for only three years when the national peak production was attained in 1925.

Logging in the Pacific Northwest was a totally different challenge to lumbermen from what they experienced in the southern states. The terrain out west was "Straight up and down, steep too," Oregon loggers said. "Down south they got it made," one veteran from the Northwest noted, "they're logging woodpecker-poles in country flat as an airfield."

There was a significant difference in timber size when comparing the two regions. Ancient forests around Valsetz probably averaged eight-foot diameter on the stump, and 150-200 feet in height. Southern pine was puny by comparison, most large trees had been harvested earlier.

The tremendous size of NW timber challenged the ingenuity of early lumbermen. At first they utilized water transport wherever possible to move the huge logs to the mills. They fell trees into, or close to water, initially using jacks and brute strength to roll the monsters into rivers, lakes or saltwater. Next came oxteams and a few horses to pull the hefty logs to water, or to a landing, over puncheon skid roads made by spacing short lengths of small-diameter logs side by side on the ground.

Steam railroad engines provided a giant leap forward for the timber industry, coupled with steam yarders and loaders that snaked logs to a central location, then loaded them onto railroad flatcars for a ride to the mill. By 1910, most NW logging oxen and horses had been put out to pasture, with the exception of a few scattered selective-logging shows using horses to save the terra firma and existing trees.

The logger's next step of progress was the development of the highlead and skyline method of bringing logs from where they fell to the landing. Yarding cables were strung in the air to eliminate dragging logs on the ground where stumps, elevation changes and by-passed trees could slow the action. Putting logs up in the air also helped save the soil surface from the gouging and furrowing formerly caused by the old dragging methods. Winter rainfall run-off delighted in using these convenient trenches to erode denuded hillsides.

After all the improvements and method changes adopted by the timber industry, the discerning among them began to look around in the late 1930's and suddenly realized maybe trees were not an inexhaustible resource after all. So, instead of their previous philosophy of "cut and run," the wise-heads began to think in long-range terms of "cut and plant." Thus, the tree farm concept was born in the Northwest.

*   *   *   *   *   *

November was the Thanksgiving issue of the Valsetz *Star* and Dorothy Anne had these tidbits to report:

"At our Thanksgiving Day dinner at the cookhouse when we played and sang, *"God Bless America,"* one hundred and sixty loggers and mill men rose to their feet and stood until we finished. They had just put the turkey on their plates, too."

"Such a funny thing happened. Mrs. T.L. Inskeep was resting in her room at the Colony Hotel at Miami Beach, Florida, when suddenly she heard over radio station WOAM, Miami, quotations from *The Valsetz Star.* It was about Mother's corsets."

"Some more letters we would like to have our readers know about:
The one from Ray Lyman Wilbur, President of *Stanford University,* and he felt badly about Jingles having his tonsils out.
From Dr. Amelia H. Rheinhardt, President of *Mills College.*
And Mrs. Percy B. Scott, of New York, managing editor of '*Guide Magazine.*'
And then the letter from Hank who finally found oil in Texas. He used to carry in wood for the loggers here and was called, '*Hank, the Bull Cook.*'
Hank has been living at the Men's Resort in Portland, and hasn't eaten a steak for a year. He will buy a new blue suit and a red tie and the old brown cords he has been wearing for twelve years he gave to a friend. He will have everything he wants only he wishes he could get his hair back."

"A nice article about *The Star* appeared in the '*Christian Science Monitor*' on October 25th.
It was entitled, '*A Window on the West,*' and was written by Donald H. Black of the '*Capitol Journal*' of Salem, Oregon. We wish to thank Mr. Black for this good story as it has brought '*The Star*' many letters and subscriptions."

"A little old lady told Mr. Frank Trower of San Francisco: 'Them's of us as ain't got no education has got to use our brains.' It would be terrible English in the sixth grade."

"President Roosevelt got stuck in the mud at Hyde Park for half-an-hour, and Henry Fromm got stuck in the Valsetz mud all night on Thanksgiving."

"Thanksgiving is over, and football is over, and the night shift is over, and school might be over at Christmas on account of there isn't any money."

"ADV. If you've got on hand some poor cheap stuff, and you wish you hadn't bought it, it's not too late, just call us up, cause Cobbs & Mitchell's got it. (Nice smooth lumber)"

"Casey Jones, who is conductor and engineer and fireman and brakeman on our funny little train out of Valsetz, stops thirty eight times on his way out to do errands for Valsetz people. Last week he stopped for half an hour and chased a whole field full of turkeys. He was trying to get one for Daddy."

"Franklin and I had pie four times Thanksgiving when nobody was looking."

"Daddy celebrated both Thanksgivings. He has been cooking Mother's meals for sixteen years. She doesn't complain."

"Fred Shaad has a new housekeeper. The first one came over the hill with a whole lot of stuff and turned right around and went back."

"Franklin lost his girl. Jingles got her."

"*The Star* is for Senator McNary for President in 1940. Everybody in Valsetz is turning into Republicans."

Virginia Green and Al Stark were married in Salem on November 24th. Glen Robinette and Bruce Robinson got married, one couple came back together again, and nobody is in jail this month."

Two Years of the Star
Autumn–December, 1939

By December, 1939, *The Valsetz Star* and its diminutive Editor, Dorothy Anne Hobson, had been in business for over two years. Her Assistant Editor, Franklin Thomas, by now was getting his newshound feet planted firmly, or as firmly as was possible in Valsetz' gooey winter mud.

Circulation of *The Star* was increasing monthly, and the mimeographing and mailing of the monthly issues was beginning to be a major task for her publisher and benefactor's office staff. Lumber broker, Herbert A. Templeton, had made Dorothy Anne an oral commitment to compose, print and distribute the output from the two journalistic kids who were now eleven-years old.

The Star was being distributed, not only across the U.S., but to several foreign countries. No less than fourteen editors of major daily newspapers across the land had "made copy" of excerpts from the kids' entertaining, newsy and satirical writings.

Following the Depression, under Republican President Herbert Hoover, U.S. voters were swinging to the Democratic party and to then-President, Franklin D. Roosevelt.

Through it all, Dorothy Anne and *The Star* remained staunch Republican supporters, but she was becoming more benevolent to Democrats. Although vacillating monthly between capitalizing or not on the names of the two political parties, she was at least fair-minded and treated them equally on the capital "R" or "D" issue.

* * * * * *

"From *The Star*, Merry Christmas to all of our readers and subscribers all over the United States and Canada, and the Phillipine Islands, and South America and Valsetz, and our one subscriber in Germany.

And we want to thank our friends and subscribers and the Republicans and Democrats for the stacks and piles of good letters they have written us this past year and encouraged us to keep on with *The Star*.

Sometimes it seems so hard and so much work that we think we will give it up and send our subscribers' money back. Franklin thinks maybe they wouldn't take the money back, but the editor is afraid they would so we will keep on.

Also we wish to thank The *Portland Oregonian*, The *Oregon Journal*, *Oregon Statesman*, The *Denver Post*, The *Philadelphia Inquirer*, The *New York Sun*, The *Los Angeles Herald*, The *Christian Science Monitor*, The *Oakland Tribune*, The *Washington, D.C. Post*, and many others for all their interest in writing such nice articles about *The Star*."

"And most of all we want to thank Mr. Herbert Templeton, President of the Templeton Lumber Co., in Portland, who is our publisher, and has given so much of his time to *The Star*. And Miss Eva Richards, in Mr. Templeton's office, who is our assistant publisher and mimeographer. Mother says it's getting about time for some more fudge."

"We are sorry about Mr. Frank W. Trower, of San Francisco. He isn't as handsome as we thought. He says the photograph of himself in the '*Hoo Hooter*' was taken 25-years ago, and his roof needs some shingling."

"The Valsetz Hill"

Over the Valsetz hill we go, what do we care about fog or snow, the winds can blow and the mud can fly, but we'll do our shopping now or die.—Over the Valsetz hill we go, what do we care if our money's low, the time is here for Yuletide lore, and we can always shop at the ten-cent store.—Over the Valsetz hill we go, what do we care if we're fast or slow, it's Christmas time and our hearts are light, if there's four in the car we sing '*Silent Night.*'"

"Anne Shannon Monroe is one of our subscribers and we are very proud of that because she writes books and things. She is writing a book at Long Beach, Washington where she can think."

"Five more people in Valsetz turned into Republicans. Everybody has forgotten Hitler, he won't have any fun Christmas."

"Mother and Daddy left December 8th on their honeymoon. Mother looked swell in her new uplift and Merle Norman eye shadow."

"And then there was a letter from Kate Smith's press agent, William P. Maloney. He sent us a little booklet that Kate Smith wrote about being patriotic, and when we ride over the hill in the mud and rain in somebody else's car, we haven't any, we sing '*God Bless America*' all the way."

"We mustn't forget the letter from Mr. Leon Stroud, who teaches science and mathematics in a small high school in Woodland, Washington. He said he was a fairly loyal Democrat, and would we please go a bit easier on the poor Democrats as they were taking an awful beating on the double Thanksgiving issue (ordained by Democratic President, FDR.)

He is terribly shocked over schools having to close all over the country on account of no money, and that billions of dollars are spent for war materials and school children deprived of their right to an education. It makes him sick."

"Merry Christmas again, and peace on earth, good will toward England and Finland and France, and America, and Mrs. Roosevelt, and maybe Italy."

LOGGER'S FARE
WINTER–JANUARY, 1940

"Come and get it," was bellowed for breakfast and supper at the logging camp messhall, while whanging on the suspended outside iron triangle with a steel rod. The clanging could be heard all around camp and it often served as a wakeup call for late sleepers.

Timber companies soon learned the surest way to keep good loggers in camp was to satisfy their need for quality vittles, served in quantity.

A fierce inter-camp rivalry often developed as various camp cooks tried to out-feed their timber competitors by stuffing their logger chowhounds. Steaks, ice cream, luscious pies and pastries baked daily were none too good for the starving-hungry woods crew.

Dorothy Anne's dad, Henry Hobson, was the cook for the Valsetz messhall and from all reports was a recognized expert in his trade. With several helpers, Hobson planned and directed preparation of the bountiful meals.

Experiencing a short stint in the Northwest timber industry (although it was more years ago than he cares to remember,) this author can attest to the sumptuous meals provided in logging camps. The breakfast fare presented huge offerings of all normal morning foods, and some that weren't. We had hotcakes, eggs, bacon, ham, toast, oatmeal, coffee, juices, milk and tea. Coming from homes of sparse grub, some men would have worked for the food alone.

The best-remembered was a giant spread called, "the spike-up table." Traditional meat sandwiches were provided to each logger in a lunch sack because of the long distances, job-site to messhall. In addition, each logger could supplement his sandwiches by taking unlimited items from the vast table array.

The selection was enormous, too varied to mention—everything from fruits, cold cuts and cheeses, thru candy bars and pastries.

Weather permitting, which it seldom did, the loggers built a big, roaring bonfire at noon, toasted the sandwiches, barbecued left-over drumsticks from the spike-up table, sometimes even filched a few extra minutes onto the half-hour lunchtime if the bull of the woods (boss) wasn't in close proximity.

The head logging camp cook had to carry five-star credentials. If he, most were men, tried to sacrifice quality to shave expenses, the finicky loggers were likely to quit en masse. Our camp cook from 'way back when had recently sold his gourmet restaurant in town and was quickly hired by the logging firm. Letting it be known through the bunkhouse telegraph system that this renowned chef was now our camp cook, enticed and retained many top-notch loggers for that organization. It just proved that a logger's faith and undying loyalty was best secured through his stomach.

* * * * * *

For the first month of the new year, Dorothy Anne reported:

"Christmas Day was very thrilling. We hurried around all day with gifts and kept saying, 'Merry Christmas' every minute.

The loggers and mill men all left for home, Hitler stuck one foot over on French soil, the gravy had too much salt, and nothing Daddy got fit."

"Happy New Year to everybody, and this is the Republican's year, and Franklin and the editor have made resolutions not to eat any more candy or pie or dressing, or sing '*Silent Night,*' or give anybody gifts for a whole year on account of getting sick Christmas. We will eat our spinach and drink milk and sing, '*God Bless America.*'"

"Senator McNary was invited to the Jackson Day dinner in Washington, but he wouldn't go. They had diamond-back terrapin soup with amontillado. He likes roast beef and apple pie."

"Daddy got Mother two boxes of cigars and a gun for Christmas."

"It's January and it seems so queer, we look outside—pussy willows are here! The robins seem so tame and jolly. We look at Mrs. Grout's door, they are eating her holly."

"ADV. Spring is coming, fix everything up.
  Order some Cobbs & Mitchell lumber,
  It's nice and smooth and doesn't cost much!"

"Mr. and Mrs. Grout, Mrs. Heydon, and Mother all hurried to Portland for fear the fur coat sales would be over."

"Jingles almost lost his girl at the dance Saturday night."

"January 15th was Czechoslovakia's New Years. Mike said so."

"Mother and Daddy had a terrible argument."

"When Donald Denno came home from the University of Oregon for Christmas vacation the girls all tried to dance with him at once. He couldn't move."

"Senator McNary doesn't want to go to the same heaven the Democrats go."

"January is the month when Robert E. Lee was born, and Uncle Ray in Alaska."

"President Roosevelt stuck his tongue out at Vice-President Garner, and Vice-President Garner kissed Mrs. Roosevelt's hand, and Elliott Roosevelt lost a tooth."

"Victor Ramey got married and Mert Archibald lost his shoes."

"Don't forget this is the year to vote for the Republicans. Two men on the bus said they would, too.

"Mr. Herbert Templeton, our publisher in Portland, is recovering from an operation. He will soon be leaving with Mrs. Templeton for a month's trip into Old Mexico where he can relax and rest and not think of a thing but lumber."

WHITE LIGHTNING AND SNOOSE
WINTER–FEBRUARY, 1940

A cottage-industry quite prevalent during the 1930-40 era was bootlegging, or producing illegal spirits through ingeniously contrived pots, tubing and moonshine apparatus. A few loggers became involved in the manufacture and distribution of "white lightning," but many more became end users.

Sensing potential problems with booze in camp at Valsetz, Herbert Templeton turned thumbs down on the sale of alcoholic beverages in the town when he bought the logging community in 1947.

Donald Denno recalls, "There was a rip-roaring saloon in Falls City that catered to Valsetz loggers. Templeton's prohibition edict didn't stop loggers with cars from patronizing the place and trundling on home with cases of beer to slake their thirst."

Even after the Volstead Act was repealed, in 1933, boot-legging continued in many sections of the U.S. With heavy taxes on "legal" spirits keeping prices at an inflated level, entrepreneurial "private distillers" could reap handsome profits from their operations. Anything illegal or immoral was bound to be in demand—and profitable. Moonshine manufacturers tried to stash their stills in tucked away valleys and remote hills, attempting to elude revenue agents who were constantly on the prowl to apprehend independent operators. It was like a friendly game of 'cops and robbers' with a few jail sentences and fines handed out to apprehended perpetrators, but nobody was hurt very badly. These 'operating expenses' were built into the cost of doing business as moonshiners calculated to have a still located and demolished by 'revenuers' from time to time. Another reason for moonshine popularity, it was said, was better taste appeal and higher octane than store-bought goods.

It has been said that a wheel would never have turned, or a tree felled in Valsetz without "Scandanavian steam," "*snoose,*" or more commonly called, *"Copenhagen"* snuff. This finely chopped and lightly moistened chewing tobacco comes in a circular box that created irre-movable, round-disc outlines on thousands of loggers' hind pockets, not to mention bulges in their lower lips. A standard in the industry a few years ago, you just weren't a he-man logger unless you had a pinch of snoose tucked away in your mouth.

Snuff-sellers were aware that their popular snoose had to be fresh. The author learned these timelines were important in the wholesale snuff business during the '40's, and probably still are.. Each can is dated at time of manufacture. A week's age—no problem; two weeks—getting borderline; three weeks—only if the customer was desperate for a "chew;" a month old—send it back where it came from.

In those days, the manufacturer, cognizant of the dating sensitivity tried many means of transportation, including air freight, to speed up shipments. Northwest loggers, mill workers, fisherpeople and anyone who developed the habit, wanted it NOW, and wanted it FRESH, and probably still do.

* * * * * *

Full of hope that it would be a "Republican Year," Dorothy Anne had this special editor's note in February, 1940: "This issue is dedi-cated to the Republicans. You will see a picture of (the Republican elephant) at the top of the page."

"We had a letter from Mr. Leon D'Emo, who is the only Republi-can in New York City. He goes shivering down the street alone and said the picking had been very poor for seven lean years. He said in his letter to us, "The Republicans have always had the business brains of this country." But we don't like to write what he said about the Democrats because so many of them subscribe to *The Star*, and besides, when they shake hands with us and smile, we like them so much."

"Also, he asked us to please not roast Governor Al Smith, as he is so well liked in New York City by both Democrats and Republicans and that he is honest and has brains. We had not planned on talking about him because he looks like Uncle Jake."

"We lost our German subscriber. We guess he got scuttled."

"Mr. Chas I. Simpson, manager of the '*Simpson Seed & Floral Co.*' of Denver, Colorado, would like to subscribe to *The Star* but said the 'New Deal' had flattened him out. It must be terrible to be 'flattened out.'"

"A letter came from Sophia McLeod Zea, of Strasburg, Va., who is eight years old and a strong Democrat. She said there were a few Republicans in Virginia but she wasn't related to any of them."

"Below is a poem written by Janice Blanchard, (Mrs. Morris Scott) of Portland, Oregon. She was in terrible dumps, and when the January *Star* arrived she wrote:
"The day was gray and the sky was blue'
And this was a miracle strangely true:
High in the sky the sun shone out,
For *The Valsetz Star* had put gloom to rout."

"Grandma Hobson is sitting up but Grandpa Hobson isn't."

"Everybody in Valsetz likes Mrs. Roosevelt. We wish she would fly over the hill sometime and land on the baseball diamond."

"We don't know if the Finns will beat the Russians.
We don't know if the budget will balance.
We don't know what Hitler will do next.
We don't know if Roosevelt will run for a third term.
We don't know anything."

"Everybody jumped into their cars and rode fast over the Valsetz road. Two cars pushed each other. They were hurrying to see, *"Gone With the Wind."*

"Jingles got his girl a Valentine with lace on it."

"We could go to New York on a free trip but Mother can't get the dye washed out of her hair."

"So many babies are being born in Valsetz that some people are getting alarmed."

"Our teachers never get any money but we won't mention it on account of Mr. Leon Stroud of Woodland, Washington, who worries."

"Levi Green had his tonsils out. Everybody in Valsetz has had something out."

"Thomas E. Dewey, who may be our next President, arrived in Portland and all the Seattle Republicans were mad because they didn't get good seats. Mother had a good seat at, *"Gone With the Wind."*

"Donald Denno's face turned red at the University of Oregon.
We heard a meadow lark. The frogs are croaking. Daddy said the Republicans will win this year. *The Star* says so too."

MRS. JINGLES
WINTER–MARCH, 1940

During the brief time spent with Ingvar and Maxine Lambert at their suburban Dallas, Oregon home, it was readily apparent that Mrs. Lambert was and always had been, "A gal with gumption," truly a card-carrying, no-nonsense, do it now, type of person.

Maxine Rowell was just twenty-one in 1940 when she met Ingvar "Jingles" Lambert at a duck pin bowling alley in Dallas when he was thirty-one years old. Duck pin bowling was an early, miniaturized version of the sport using smaller pins, and small balls without finger holes.

"I thought bowling a score of 256 would show her how good I was," Ingvar recalls with a grin. "She turned right around and bowled a 265," he said, a proud smile breaking across his large-featured face.

"We've always done a lot of things together," Maxine replied. "We both enjoy golfing and usually go to the course together."

"Yes, she's a darned good golfer, too," Lambert said. "But I've got one up on her. I once made a hole in one and she hasn't beat that."

"At least not yet," Maxine said, beaming her competitive smile.

In seeking her thoughts and opinions on life and how to live it, Maxine shared these observations: "I think people should make lists of accomplishments and experiences they wish to fulfill during their lifetime. Not everyday, mundane kinds of things, but unusual, maybe even demanding objectives that would require extra effort."

"Is that something you've done?" I asked.

"Yes, I have," the petite Oregon housewife, mother of three, admitted. "And I still have a few experiences on my 'to-do' list. Some I've done and crossed off."

"Like what?" I asked.

Just a hint of a smile tweaked across her face as she gazed off into the distance. "I'd always wanted to fly in a helicopter. I did it and thoroughly enjoyed the ride."

"How about giving me an example of one of your unfulfilled experiences?"

"I have one I wouldn't want to share with you, it's kind of silly," the octogenarian said.

"It's not silly if you've put it on your list," I responded.

"Well, you would think it's very unusual."

"Sounds interesting," I replied. "You've awakened my curiosity."

"O.K., you asked for it. I've always yearned to go skinny- dipping in a hot tub," Maxine finally admitted. "My daughter, Laura has a tub and I've told her I'm going to come over someday when there's nobody else around and fulfill my ambition." She grinned at her husband, Jingles, exactly as I envisioned her smiling at Jing that day at the duck pin bowling alley back in 1940.

*   *   *   *   *   *

The Valsetz Star of March, 1940 reported:

"Jingles got his girl back. It was on account of the lace on the Valentine."

Another Republican elephant picture graced *The Valsetz Star*'s March, 1940 issue. "The picture at the top of the page is a Republican reading, '*The Valsetz Star*.' The elephant is leaning against a tree that belongs to Cobbs & Mitchell."

" We had a nice letter from Mr. Leslie Chandler, of New York City. He said if we ever go to New York he will take us to a restaurant and order a large piece of apple pie with two scoops of ice cream. Some of the Democrats are so nice!"

"We are very proud of a letter from Mr. James D. Regan, head of the Groton School, of Groton, Mass., where President Roosevelt and all his sons graduated. He read about *The Star* in the *'New York Herald Tribune.'*"

"Confucius say: People who read Valsetz *Star* turn into Republicans."

"A woman from Lawrence, Indiana, wrote us to BEWARE, that Christ is coming soon. We don't know what to do."

Maxine and Ingvar Lambert on Thanksgiving Day, 1999, as they celebrated his 90th birthday. The Dallas couple will honor their 60th wedding anniversary in June, 2001. (Photo courtesy the Lamberts)

"We will soon have the solid south behind us on account of so many subscribers, and New York, too. We hope President Roosevelt won't mind."

"Mr. Herbert Templeton, our publisher in Portland, who with Mrs. Templeton has just returned from a vacation in Old Mexico, came to visit us. While in Valsetz Mr. Templeton was invited to the school and gave a very interesting talk on their trip. We clapped and clapped."

"ADV. Mr. Bert Yeager, of 11 Briancroft Road, Toronto, Canada, who is one of our subscribers, read our ad in *The Star* and he will ask for Cobbs & Mitchell lumber when he orders his supply next month.

We hope everybody will do the same. It's nice and smooth!"

"Mrs. Ann Heydon said she was fighting Indians on the Valsetz Hill when Daddy and the American Legion were winning the World War over at Vancouver Barracks."

"Valsetz had 31-inches of rainfall in February."

"Jingles got his girl back. It was on account of the lace on the Valentine."

"Nobody got in jail in March."

"Grandpa Hobson passed away in Salem on February 26th. Grandma Hobson is still in bed."

"Mrs. Roosevelt was resting behind a palm tree in Florida. She paid the rent for a whole month and only stayed two weeks."

"Best-dressed men in America: Mr. Paul McNutt, Albert Vanderbilt, and Cy Cyphert, our sawyer."

"Mrs. Edsel P. Ford, of San Francisco, can't understand why Donald Denno's face turned red at the University of Oregon. She said in her letter: "My husband and I were both graduated from the University of Oregon, and our faces didn't turn red." But she said they had two red-headed children."

"Hitler shouted and yelled again on the 24th."

"James Roosevelt got a divorce and Leonard got married to Bernice."

"Daddy is trying to find a place for his vacation this summer where his stomach won't get any bigger."

SAWMILL EVOLUTION
SPRING–APRIL, 1940

As chainsaws, gasoline and diesel power revolutionized logging, so, too, did steam-powered circular and bandsaws bring efficiency and high-volume cutting to early Northwest sawmills.

Man first discovered that trees could be fashioned into flat boards several eons ago. The earliest, "sawmill," consisted of a two-man-powered whipsaw. One pulled the saw through a log from above on a raised platform while his less fortunate partner pulled the saw from below. The lower operator received a generous and constant shower of sawdust for his efforts.

Then one day, we can suppose, one of the whipsaw operators, while nursing sore muscles and combing sawdust from his hair, watched the great power of water in a fast-moving stream. And he dreamed, oh how he dreamed, of how he could harness that power to saw his logs.

During the second-half of the nineteenth century man devised a slow but certain method to harness water-power. Waterfalls or flumes were controlled to turn waterwheels—not very speedy, but they worked. With belts and gears the circular saw blades could attain speeds of 500-800 rpm. The cutting blades looked something like the round blades on our table saws or hand-held power saws, although much bigger and much slower.

When lumbermen first began producing boards from the giant California redwoods and humongous NW trees, they realized that a single, circular sawblade had never been invented that would slice-up ten or twelve-foot diameter logs. Once again, ingenuity took over and two circular saws were installed on the head-rig, one above the other.

In the early days of sawmilling some operators actually preferred logs of three or four-foot diameter instead of the old-growth ten-footers. The puny logs were also easier for the oxen to drag out of the woods.

Mill owners who disliked the unorthodox one-above-the-other circular saw arrangement began tinkering with another method, the continuous bandsaw. These skinny, narrow saw blades, some up to thirty or forty feet in length, seemed to be a cut above the old-fashioned circulars. Only problem, millmen had a devil of a time trying to run the floppity things in a straight line. And when they came loose and snapped into one long blade, as early models had a tendency to do, the darned things banged and slashed around the mill like an angry snake, not caring who, or what they bit.

Around the turn of the century, when Great Lakes speculator, Frederick Weyerhaeuser, consumated the largest single land purchase in U.S. history, steam-power was being utilized for lumbering muscle. Mr. Weyerhaeuser, associated with eleven other Minnesota and Wisconsin investors, reportedly bought 900,000 acres of NW timberlands for $6 million. The 65-year old German immigrant built his huge timber company that today manages 5.3 million acres of forestlands, doing $11 billion in annual sales.

The lumber industry finally overcame their obstacles, developed sophisticated improvements such as electronic controls, and went on to cut thousands of board feet per hour in their modern sawmills.

*   *   *   *   *   *

In Valsetz winter was on the way out and Dorothy Anne heralded the new season: "It's spring and everything is white with blossoms, and the air smells so sweet. But we never saw the like—they are fighting over in Europe and the fallers and buckers are fighting here, and the Democrats and the Republicans are fighting everywhere, and the kids at school are all sticking their tongues out."

"The picture (on the *Star's* front page) is a Republican marching at the head of the band. He looks like he thinks he is smart, but he doesn't. He just thinks he will be elected."

"We have received a letter from Mr. Alfred E. Smith, who was once governor of New York, and he would like to see us if we come to New York, and we can ride all the way to the top of the Empire State Building."

"Daddy is afraid President Roosevelt will be elected again on account of his charm. We wish the Republicans would hurry up and get some charm so they could get elected."

"We are proud of a letter from Mr. James A. Farley, who is postmaster general. He wishes us well and dashes his name off in green ink. He isn't a Republican."

"Mrs. James A. Young, of Centralia, Wash., thinks the Republicans will come racing home with *The Valsetz Star* behind them."

"To the Republicans:
We would like you to know just how serious we've been,
And how much has been said just for fun;
And we'll forgive you everything else that you do,
If you'll only make a home run."

"Our teachers haven't had any pay yet. Some of them are gathering dandelions for greens."

"Mrs. Roosevelt said, "Golly," but it isn't a bad word."

"Bill Byers landed the longest fish here Saturday, and Germany landed in Norway on Monday."

"ADV. Mr. J.R. McKenzie, one of our subscribers in Moose Jaw, Sask., read our ad, and wants to order a carload of Shop Pine from Cobbs & Mitchell, but we don't have any."

"Will somebody please tell us how the Republicans can get some more glamour?"

A typical large Douglas fir tree accommodating five loggers seated in the undercut. The two men on each side of the tree are standing on springboards which provided a working platform for sawing and chopping the high undercut.

"Daddy found a place to spend his vacation, but the manager said he built stomachs up, he didn't take them down."

"The Valsetz baseball team will open the season with a game with The Dalles next Sunday, April 20th."

"Mr. Hall Templeton came to Valsetz to fish on opening day, but didn't get one. But he had a nice boat ride."

"Curtis Grout got a new car. The Thomas' got a new car. The hens are starting to set again. Mrs. Denno has six toes on one foot, and we've stopped taking cod liver oil."

"Mr. James D. Regan, of Groton School, (President Roosevelt's school) is called 'Senior Master.'"

"We hope some day we will have enough money to pay Mr. Templeton, our publisher in Portland, for all the free work he has done for us."

"Confucius said he wishes he hadn't said anything in the first place."

"Miss Betty Starr, daughter of our Vice-President, Mr. C.L. Starr, has been chosen May Queen at Willamete University in Salem."

"Franklin, the Assistant Editor, is getting awfully tired of the New Deal."

"Grandma Hobson wants to live long enough to see the Republicans in charge again."

"Weather Forecast: Getting ready for rain again."

HERBERT A. TEMPLETON
SPRING–MAY, 1940

Dorothy Anne's benefactor and family friend, Herbert A. Templeton, was president of the '*Valsetz Lumber Co.*' prior to stepping down to become chairman of the board in 1957. At that time his son,

Hall Templeton, took over dad's position as president.

When the diminutive Missy Hobson whispered to Templeton, in 1937, that she was going to be editor of a new newspaper, *The Valsetz Star*, he volunteered to publish it for her. The lumber dealer's office staff typed the mimeograph stencil and printed the ever-increasing number of copies each month.

Although Templeton volunteered all these services and undoubtedly never charged the tabloid tots for his publishing efforts, the benefits certainly were advantageous to both of them.

In the April, 1940 issue of *The Star*, Dorothy Anne wrote: "Each month he (Templeton) buys 250 copies of *The Star* and sends them free to lumber companies and other places." This distribution would have benefitted both parties. Recipients would not soon forget the unusual name of Valsetz, either for its newspaper, or for its 2 X 4's.

During the paper's four year reign, Templeton arranged for many social events and appearances for Dorothy Anne and her mother, not only in Portland, but across the country. In 1941, he orchestrated, then chaperoned Dorothy and Mrs. Hobson to the Hollywood radio studio of Gabriel Heatter's national radio program, *"We The People,"* where Dorothy was interviewed. The threesome attended celebrity-ranked events while in California, all arranged or paid for by Herbert Templeton.

The lumberman and his wife, Ruth, raised four children in Portland and both were quite active in various civic organizations. They reportedly bestowed a $1 million endowment to Lewis and Clark College in 1961.

We would think that Templeton cherished his memories of Dorothy Anne, *The Valsetz Star*, and the tight little logging community where he often visited. He passed away in 1969 at the age of 86-years, having been in the lumber business for sixty-years.

*   *   *   *   *   *

The May, 1940 issue of the Valsetz *Star* predicted: "The worst rain we ever had."

"Daddy said Hitler is drunk with power, and two loggers drank some raisin juice."

"When the Republican National Convention is held in Philadelphia next month, President Roosevelt is going to travel all over the country waving his hat and smiling so nobody will pay any attention to the Republicans. We wish we could do something."

"Daddy has decided to keep his stomach on account of protecting his country."

"President Roosevelt's mother had the stomach-ache."

"Mr. Cal Woolley, a Valsetz logger, sent to St. Louis for his teeth and they fit swell. He can even crack hazel nuts. He used to drink "Old Crow" but now he has money in the bank."

"Mr. Thomas, our superintendent, flew east in a plane and Mrs. Thomas got scared and went on the train."

"Mr. and Mrs. Thomas returned from St. Paul, Chicago, Michigan and California, each driving their own car. They didn't have any when they left"

"Mr. C.L. Starr, our Vice-President, came to Valsetz followed by twelve strong Republicans. They were his guests at dinner."

"Mr. Ethan Allen, a seventy-three year old Republican who lives alone and likes it on an island in Waldon, Wash., said to tell Daddy that if Congress will give Mr. Roosevelt money enough the Republicans can't beat him even if the candidate had a rabbit's foot in his

Longtime Valsetz resident, Donald Denno, reviews a 1984 Sunday supplement printed by the Portland Oregonian that described the rise and fall of the isolated timber community. (Author photo)

pocket, a horseshoe nailed on his breast, and a four-leaf clover in his buttonhole. He can make cookies, biscuits, and jelly."

"Members of the Bridge Club have been working on a very beautiful quilt, which they will raffle off and give the money to the Parent-Teachers to be used for the school. We will thank them as soon as we get the money."

"Franklin, the Assistant Editor, is mad. He is so mad he turned pale. It's on account of Hitler. He (Franklin, not Hitler,) has started taking cod liver oil again."

"FLASH: At the last minute the Valsetz teachers got all their pay for the whole year in one big pile.
Miss Vanhining hurried to Portland with a suitcase full."

Valsetz Inventory
Spring–June, 1940

Several of the Valsetz *Star*'s subscribers had requested a more detailed description of the town and what people did in Valsetz. Always sensitive to her readers, Dorothy Anne responded:

"Mr. Charles A. Pecker, one of our New England subscribers, Marblehead, Mass., would like us to give our readers a little more information about the town of Valsetz, such as the population, climate, how many trains, and buses, schools, churches and movies.

The population of Valsetz is 800, and we are fifteen miles down the canyon to the Pacific Ocean, but you have to go around.

We have no buses, and only one train, but there is no use to talk on it because nobody can hear.

One winding mountain road and if you go lickety split over it you'll land in the ditch.

There are six hundred cars (?), three hundred refrigerators, fifty-five davenports, and one Sunday school.

One fortune teller, (Mrs. Fee); one beauty parlor, no picture show, no bank, but Mother and Mr. Grout will cash your checks if they aren't too big; one restaurant—Daddy; two unions, one glee club; one post office with venetian blinds; ninety eight circulating heaters; four strawberry patches; one bridge club; one barber shop; one newspaper (*The Star!*); one sawmill; one handle factory; two timekeepers and a half; four dressmakers; eighteen cows and no beer parlor.

One doctor, 800 radios; one library; one baseball club; 600 Republicans and 22 Democrats; One CCC camp but it isn't here yet. One high school, one grade school; six teachers with no pay, and 500 dogs.

*   *   *   *   *   *

In the June issue of *The Star*, Dorothy Anne continued with her description and inventory of Valsetz.

"We are completely surrounded by five billion feet of timber and shortly after Columbus discovered America those trees were little saplings and are now so large that some of them contain 20,000-feet of lumber, which is enough to build a large modern home."

"Throughout those timbered mountains are miles of truck roads with gravel one foot deep over which we bring our logs to the pond. We hope Mussolini and Hitler don't read about this."

"Valsetz is twenty-two years old and has an elevation of 1,150 feet."

"The sawmill manufactures two hundred thousand feet of lumber a day and one million feet a week. And the mill pond covers seven hundred and twenty acres."

"In the basement of the sawmill is a handle factory which manufactures 15,000 handles a day. The handles are made of slabs which formerly was waste lumber, and are shipped all over the world to make broom handles for women to sweep the floors."

"If Valsetz is invaded by Mussolini and Hitler, Mr. Leonard, President of the handle factory, will furnish all the women with broom handles to chase away the invaders."

"Two loggers and three millmen proposed to our teacher, Miss Vanhining, but she took her suitcase full of money and ran to Portland."

"It looks like God has left us all alone to fight,
But we'll keep on making bombs, and things will come out right.
P.S. But we will keep on praying too."

"Mr. Templeton, our publisher in Portland, and Mrs. Templeton, left for a months trip to New York to see Camilla."

"We are standing behind President Roosevelt and Kate Smith in these awful times and we think the Republicans had better too."

"We don't mind if people write and tell us what's wrong with us."

"We have 800 (?) automobiles in Valsetz and one Trojan Horse."

"One man took a sock at his wife, and mother sent for two boxes of shells."

"ADV. And don't waste time in doubt and wonder,
Order now our nice smooth lumber."

"This issue is dedicated to the Republican National Convention held in Philadelphia on the twenty-fourth of this month. We hope they will choose a good Republican candidate because we think the next President of the United States will be a Republican."

"When we started *The Star* two-and-a-half years ago we believed in Republicans and kindness; we still believe in Republicans but we've stopped being so kind on account of collections and Hitler."

"It's June and there is still no peace in the world and it's hard to be funny and cheerful, but we don't think Hitler will win everything and we think the Republicans will win in November, and we will keep publishing *The Star* because the subscribers want us to. One subscriber said *The Star* gives him 'joy and happiness,' and one woman wrote that some months her sides, 'just simply split.'"

"Mr. Ralph E. Williams, Republican National Committeeman who died recently, was one of our subscribers and had paid for *The Star* for two years. If any of our subscribers know the address of Mrs. Williams will they please send it to us so we can send her *The Star* for a year."

ADOLPH SCHICKLGRUBER
SUMMER–JULY, 1940

Dorothy Anne and her sidekick, Franklin, seemed obsessed with the German warlord, Adolph Hitler. Nearly every issue of *The Star* contained comments about the dictator's latest appearance, speech or military action. Most of those comments, understandably, were not complimentary.

The kids, and most Americans, had seen newsreel footage of the German army's blitzkrieg attacks on smaller European countries and atrocities they committed on helpless victims in concentration camps. People began referring to Hitler as "*Schicklgruber.*"

Failing to graduate from high school, in 1919 the rogue joined the National Socialist German Worker's party, or shortened, the Nazi party. He went on to hold several positions with the Nazis, topped off by organizing an unsuccessful revolt for which he was handed a five-year prison sentence. While in the pokey, he wrote his infamous book, "*Mein Kampf,*" through his secretary, also infamous, Rudolph Hess.

German President Hindenburg, (famous for having a zeppelin named after him,) defeated Adolph's run for Germany's top spot, but then el presidente bestowed the title of chancellor on the little man with the Charlie Chaplin black moustache.

In the mid-thirties the German populace was disheartened by many social events occurring in the fatherland. They had lost WWI and felt oppressed by the stringent treaties thrust upon them. Their economy was near collapse, unemployment was rampant, inflation was limiting their purchasing power—in short, things just weren't going peaches and cream for Germany.

But suddenly, there came a man who claimed to be their savior. Walking over lesser government officials, Hitler quickly rose to power. Der Fuhrer gained leadership of the armed forces by executing some of their top military officers and exiling others to forced-work sauerkraut factories.

Once in control, Hitler's forces steamrolled through much of Europe and tried to bomb Britain into submission. He formed an alliance with Italy and Japan, planning to conquer the world. But *Schicklgruber* made his biggest mistake when he declared war on the U.S.A.. His second blunder was attacking Russia in the winter of 1941 without furnishing his soldiers with mittens and wool socks. (As Dorothy Anne would have described it.)

Hitler's wild dreams of world domination came to an end in the Berlin bunker in 1945 when he placed a pistol to his head and his mistress, Eva Braun, gulped down cyanide pills. Valsetz and the world rested easier after that fortuitous episode.

*   *   *   *   *   *

Happiness reigned supreme at the general offices of the *Valsetz Star* newspaper (Dorothy Anne's playhouse) as they celebrated news of the Presidential campaign.

"This is the happiest issue we have ever had published on account of Wendell Willkie, who used to fry eggs and wash dishes so he could go to college, and Charley McNary, who waited on table at Stanford University and has a farm only 40-miles from Valsetz and he likes prunes and nuts—not people—fruit!"

"Once two years ago we got discouraged about the Republicans, but we never mentioned it. We still believed in them and stood behind them, but now we are standing right up in front with them, and we won't send a copy of *The Star* to President Roosevelt this month because he will feel so blue."

"A letter came to us from Mr. Frank W. Trower, a San Francisco lumberman, and one of our oldest subscribers (not in years), and he thinks *The Valsetz Star* did some fine work keeping up the courage of the Republicans during the dark days of defeat, and with the east and west united on the Republican ticket we will have a united party and a real United States.

He also said there was an Irishman in the San Francisco earthquake who said he was thrown out of bed and 'lost his conscience right away.'"

"The Democrats are winking and smiling,
 And getting an awful kick
 But if they ever beat Wendell and Charley,
 They'll have to be awful slick."

"Daddy and Wendell Willkie and Dave Oller have never owned a car."

"A man in Ohio wrote and said the Republicans pulled the only smart thing they have done in eight years, and that nobody in God's world can beat Wendell and Charley and Jo."

"Barbara Dorr, Editorial Department of 'Sunset Magazine,' wrote and asked us what do we mean by one-half timekeeper. It's Mother!"

This 1928 photo of Valsetz shows the barren, logged-off hills above the town. A few of the many company-owned family homes are in the foreground, bachelor bunkhouses, left rear; drying and loading sheds, right rear. (Photo courtesy Oregon Historical Society)

The Valsetz lumber mill was operating full speed in December, 1950, owned at that time by Herbert Templeton. The mill pond is in the upper left corner, bunk houses and family homes in the foreground. (Photo courtesy Oregon Historical Society)

"We had another letter from Ethan Allen of Waldron, Wash. He is quite old and has been ill, but he hopes God and a doctor in Bellingham can keep him on this side of the Great Divide in the Sunset Mountains so he can vote for Willkie and McNary."

"ADV. 'The Prairie Lumberman,' a Canadian lumber
magazine, said: 'He who builds a house of green lumber will soon have open house.' Phone in your order now for Cobbs & Mitchell's nice smooth finished lumber."

"A two-week Summer Bible School was in session during June."

"Mrs. Hayden hasn't a gun left and everybody is making jam. The Wests went to Seattle, the Williamsons went to Montana, Jingles went to Canada, Bill Mitchell went to Michigan, and Mother and Daddy went to sleep."

"While our publishers were away on vacation, Mr. Hall Templeton rolled up his sleeves and published the June copy of 'The Star.' We thought it was very good except the little G.O.P. elephant wasn't very clear."

"The yards are all dried up and the water is getting low. Mr. Shunke will go to the Fair to see Sally again, and the baseball team is almost in the league. The hill road is a cloud of dust, and we have only had six fires this year."

"Weather Forecast: No rain until September."

CASH CROP TREES
SUMMER–AUGUST, 1940

Oregon's bread-and-butter tree had always been the stately Douglas fir, by far the king of the woods, the leader for quality and quantity.

But other species have also been important to the lumber industry's economic growth. The Northwest's western red cedar has been adapted to a multitude of uses including lumber, shingles, shakes and just about any application necessitating durability. Cedar logs have been unearthed following decades of contact with soil, and found to be in perfect condition. Much of the shake roofing industry obtains raw material from salvaged logs and stumps left by early loggers who by-passed or wasted cedar.

Pacific Northwest stands of coniferous spruce trees were vital in building early airplanes. The skeletal framework of the initial "Jennies" was built from spruce wood, highly prized for its strength and lightweight. During WWI when airplane production was vital to the U.S. stand against Germany's aggression, the army sent teams of spruce loggers into NW forests to select the best quality trees for the war effort. With later experiments in alloys of various metals, aluminum and strong, lightweight elements were found to be superior to wood in airplane construction.

Alder was long overlooked as having any commercial value until the 1930's. It's only use, as discovered by many westerners, was for burning in cookstoves, space heaters and fireplaces, but also ideal for smoking fish and wild game.

It was discovered that green alder, properly dried, becomes hard and strong, ideal for furniture manufacturing. Long considered one of the Northwest's most prolific trash trees, alder is fast growing, attaining saw log size in less than twenty-years. Alder is classified as a hardwood even though it is quite soft in it's green form. Two of it's redeeming factors are easy accessibility and low cost, both a boon to the furniture-making industry.

So, while "Doug fir" is king, other trees in the Pacific Northwest forests have a commercial value and contribute substantially to the lumber industry's cash registers, and most importantly, their payrolls.

*   *   *   *   *   *

Back at Valsetz in August, 1940, Dorothy Anne was being scolded by the Democrats and her peers:

"Mr. Frank Wendel, of Lyman, Wyoming, thinks we are terrible, and that the Republicans are awful, and that Wendell Willkie is dreadful, and he hopes we will print this in *The Star*.

My! he said such things! That the last issue of *The Star* was smeared with limburger cheese, and that the Republican party is making a laughing stock of itself, and that Willkie is bloated and his pants are too big, and he doesn't know how to spend money, and that Wall Street will soon have it all.

That we should worry about President Roosevelt getting mad because we didn't send him the July *Star*, and he would just consider the source, and that if Willkie didn't know enough to buy a car then he surely couldn't expect to manage state affairs.

He closed his letter by saying, "Don't worry, poor girl, you no doubt was paid a nice sum of money for that stuff in *The Valsetz Star*."

But, gosh! We don't get any pay only our one dollar for yearly subscriptions, and everything we say comes out of our heads, and Mother thought it was all swell and that it showed spirit, but she didn't believe a word of it.

Daddy laughed until the rafters in our low-ceiling house shook. Some of them are getting loose anyway."

"Don't forget to pray on September 8th. Keep thinking of Willkie and McNary."

"The donkeys look so funny now, we hope they don't get mad,
But the G.O.P.'s will beat them, things look awful bad!"

"We have many subscribers in New York City, and the east, and we would like them to know that Salem, Oregon is the home of Charley McNary, and is only an hour's ride from Valsetz. We also have a letter from Mr. McNary in our files written long before he ever thought of being vice-president."

"We think Mrs. Willkie is pretty."

"Mother said she could remember men logging with oxen, but never with cats."

"President Roosevelt said he was poorer now than when he went in the White House, and Hitler wishes he could have peace."

"ADV. Lumber sales are getting good, and prices going high.
Order now some C & M, don't let this slip by.
Order Cobbs & Mitchell's nice smooth lumber now."

"Jingles went to Canada on a month's vacation trip and ran into a cyclone. He had never seen one before. People were running in every direction. He thought it was a pageant and drove along the highway so he could see it. Pretty soon his car was lifted off the earth. Everything turned black, and he will never go back."

"The loggers had a picnic. Everything free—ice cream, cheese, pop, dancing, park your car, and beer."

"Uncle Sam wishes our boys would all get ready to fight and save us. Franklin is taking vitamin "D" again."

"Donald Denno and Bill Fraser are working their way through college like Wendell Willkie and Charley McNary."

"Daddy hasn't any sons, but he wishes his daughter would be an ambulance driver and Mother would wrap bandages so he could stay home. Once he went, though."

"The Grouts left on a trip to see Crater Lake, and Susan."

"August has been a very exciting month in Valsetz. First, our swimming hole dried up. A snake took one of our goldfish. Mrs. Heydon had her tonsils out. Daddy gained four more pounds. One dog went mad. And Mother has gas on her stomach."

"Weather Forecast: Clouds. Looks like rain."

THE ROAD TO NOWHERE
SUMMER–SEPTEMBER, 1940

Today's drive from Falls City towards Valsetz can be (a) muddy and sloppy during the rainy season, Jan. - Dec.; (b) a dusty experience during dry weather with near zero visibility; (c) on a perfect day half-way between (a) and (b) it can be somewhat enjoyable—watch out for behemoth-size log trucks, they own the road.

If the day is pleasant, the scenery is well worth the trip. All phases of managed tree farming on Boise Cascade's Valsetz Tree Farm can be viewed—harvestable stands of second/third growth timber, primarily Douglas fir; hillsides (Kansans call them mountainsides) of young, planted trees that will be logged upon attaining maturity; and some hillsides that look to be barren after being logged in recent years. Many clear-cuts appearing to be nude might actually have been planted with young seedlings too small to see without a closer look.

Depending on whose numbers you accept, the drive to Valsetz will be 13, 15 or 16 miles. My speedo registered 16-miles but it was a wet, sloppy day and perhaps my car suffered wheel-slippage in the slick spots, giving a false mileage reading. Far from straight, the road is as crooked as an Arabian used-camel merchant.

Please, don't let me mislead you. Short of risking a jail sentence, nobody actually goes to Valsetz anymore. First off, there is no Valsetz, remember it was all crunched up by machine and torched back in '84.

Prior to that, when Valsetz was still granted a niche on this earth, visitors were greeted by a rustic, handcrafted log sign, "Welcome to Valsetz," affixed with the Boise-Cascade logo. There is still a sign, just a bit short, I assume, of the former townsite. It's not exactly a "welcome" sign. In fact, I had the eerie feeling that a rifle-toting guard was watching me from the bushes. The sign emphatically states, "NO TRESPASSING."

The fine-print alludes to all the nasty things that the owners would do to anyone continuing beyond the sign; a-foot, a-car, or on horseback.

There was a sturdy iron gate at the sign but it was open to allow logging truck access. Several passed as I contemplated my burning desire to visit the former townsite. I didn't go into the "no-man's zone," having no desire to out-Boise, Boise-Cascade. I never had the courage to be a coward.

Log-loads on the trucks I saw certainly did not resemble old-growth of the 1920's. The new breed of Valsetz loggers are now cutting Southern-style, woodpecker poles, evidently the only type of timber remaining in Dorothy Anne's former backyard.

*　*　*　*　*　*

In the September, 1940 edition of *The Star*, Dorothy Anne told of her adventure to Senator McNary's home near Salem.

"We had such a time this month.

We rode out in the press bus to Senator McNary's farm at Fircone, and had salmon cooked in the ground by Henry Thiele, who is a chef in Portland. His stomach is the same size as Daddy's.

As we drove past the orchard we saw three Democrats stealing Senator McNary's filberts. They ran when they saw us.

You never saw so many Republicans eating salmon. We just filled our plates real high and nobody cared where we sat.

We were real thrilled when Senator McNary sat right close to us, and an army officer who was simply covered with gold braid, said once there was a private in the army who said, "The major gives the captain hell, and the captain gives the lieutenant hell, and the lieutenant gives the sergeant hell, and everybody gives me hell, and I want to go home."

He said that right in front of us!

After lunch everybody walked around and talked. Joe Martin, chairman of the Republican National Committee, kept talking and laughing with a lady in blue—his wife couldn't come.

Governor Stassen, of Minnesota, was holding a lady's hand. We passed a group of Republicans who were swearing something fierce. Mother said, "Oh, well, they are probably thinking about the Democrats."

"If only we could think sometimes, that things would all come out
Just the way we want them to, but we guess they will no doubt."

"We received a letter and subscription from Memory Roberts, who writes ads on Sperry breakfast foods with Sam Hays, and she said she is thirty-four years old outside and about ten years old inside. Franklin thinks she must be forty-four then. We will find out in the seventh grade this year."

"President Roosevelt and Willkie are both getting mad, and Tom Allen says, 'Busoms are coming back.'"

"Hitler jumped up and down last week and shook his fist at England and shouted, "We'll come over and wipe you off the slate." The kids in the seventh grade talk that way, too."

"Mr. Sather, a druggist, of Silverton, Oregon, wrote and said, "We think Willkie will be elected, don't we?"

"Anita has a guimpe."

"ADV. Buy your lumber from Cobbs & Mitchell before prices go up. It's nice and smooth."

"Things have been very busy and exciting in Valsetz this month.
They put big lights up on the hill and haul logs all night. And we have a new puppy who is named, 'Smudge,' but Mother is mad at him on account of what happened on the living room rug."

"Jingles got a new sweater on account of the new teacher and Dave got married, and Dick got married, and Mrs. Grout is making pickles and Marjorie Thomas sold enough Christmas cards to get her wooden shoes, and Mother sent Daddy's pajamas to the laundry with his Willkie button on."

"Mr. and Mrs. Guy West have left Valsetz.
The ladies of the bridge club gave Mrs. West a lovely silver dish.

She cried. It was a good dish, though."

"Principal Roth: 'If Napoleon were alive today what would he be doing?'
Franklin Thomas: 'He would be drawing his old age pension.'"

"School opened Monday, the 16th, and is all nice and shiney inside with new paint on account of the quilt."

"Jingles took his sweater back on account of the new teacher getting married at the last minute."

"Bruce C. Dein, one of our Pennsylvanians, said, 'The fine spirit of the Valsetz *Star* has inspired my friends and me to fight for the cause."

RIDING THE SKUNK
AUTUMN–OCTOBER, 1940

During Valsetz' early days, the only way in or out of town short of shank's mare, was via the Valley and Siletz Railroad which connected with the Southern Pacific at Independence. Later, the narrow 16-mile, white knuckle driving road, Falls City to Valsetz, offered a second route through the hills. It became the Valsetz road, officially Polk County road #8610.

In addition to hauling logs, the iron horse offered passenger service, originally charged at about four-cents per mile. Loggers and millmen could whoop it up in Portland's Burnside district, jump onto the S.P., transfer to the V & S.R. at Independence and ride the rails all the way into camp for about two bucks a head.

The railroad experience was a noisy, rattling jaunt in a quasi-passenger car later driven by engineer, conductor and brakeman, P.W. "Casey" Jones, and dubbed "The Skunk," the rail car, not "Casey." Another rail car, painted yellow, was called, what else, "The Bumblebee." A third was the "Chatterbox."

Built by leaps and sections, the railroad construction had begun in Independence in 1912, moving along southwest to the tiny burgh of Hoskins, where Cobbs & Mitchell had built a lumber mill. Here the line turned northwest for fifteen miles, partially climbing Fanno Ridge, and arrived at the edge of the Luckiamute burn in 1917. The Michigan millmen constructed a small camp, called camp #1, at the end of the track, which was about four miles east of the eventual Valsetz townsite.

The Valsetz population was around 800 folks in December, 1937, with over 200 kids attending school. Polk County road #8610 was upgraded from a single cowpath in 1968 to a super highway where two cows could walk abreast. Compared with the railroad, the improved vehicle road could have been described as a commuter-friendly, non-alternative.

With a better road and pickup trucks becoming popular, some loggers and millworkers began living "outside," and commuting to the woods and mills. During later years, the local vernacular insisted that loggers drove "rigs," not pickups.

Originally built by timbermen, Cobbs & Mitchell, the Valley and Siletz Railroad fell into obsolescence when diesel and gasoline log trucks could do a better job for less money. The tracks and ties were dismantled, rail cars and lokeys, including the venerable #104 retired, or placed in railroad museums.

*　*　*　*　*　*

In Valsetz the weather forecast by Dorothy and Franklin: "Gentle rains followed by hard ones."

"We got an awful stab in the back. A man from Philadelphia who 'relies on our honesty,' not to mention his name, says *The Valsetz Star* is 'crude and crusty.' That it shows neither grown up intelligence nor a child's perspicacity, and that our choice of a presidential candidate is on the level with one who neither reads, studies, or has any brains. Also he said we gave him a pain.

We guess he needs *'Carter's Little Liver Pills.'*"

"We think maybe the world will come out all right. We aren't sure."

"Mussolini and Hitler are terribly worried. They met in Brenner Pass and whispered and whispered. People who whisper are very rude and don't always turn out well."

"Mr. Templeton, our publisher in Portland, has not called on us for some time. He is very busy selling lumber. He flies east and everything."

"The sun is shining this 15th day of October. Down by the dam where we walked this afternoon a small pert bluebird flew from a red-leafed maple tree and followed us. We sat on a log and it waited beside us.

When we crossed the dam and went into the hills it followed us again, and down the trail on the other side for two miles it flew quietly along. On our return it flew low ahead of us until coming within sight of the mill when it suddenly flew across the lake and disappeared over the ridge of the hills.

When we returned home we looked in our bird book to see if we could find some meaning. Daddy said it means Willkie will be elected."

"We received a pamphlet from the manager of the House of Santanakaran, Narsapur, West Godavari District, in South India, and it tells how to have babies if you haven't any."

"A subscriber in Denver, Colorado, says it doesn't take long to read *The Valsetz Star*, but it sticks to his ribs."

"Will our readers please notice that the word, 'American,' ends in, 'I can.' It gives us courage."

"Our budget never balances any more on account of Mother not being a home-maker. She is campaigning for Willkie."

"We sat in a picture show and some people booed at President Roosevelt. We do not boo at our president of the United States. We do not boo at anybody. We sat very dignified."

"A subscriber in Boston, Mass. thinks *The Valsetz Star* is 'chuck full' of charm and will we please keep it up."

"ADV. We think the time has arrived to open your eyes,
And your hearts and your purse as well, and buy C & M lumber—
It sure is a hummer, and, we have millions of feet to sell."

"Mrs. Ann Heydon has a new front porch on the post office."

"Mrs. Frank Morovec, who draws the little G.O.P.'s for *The Star*, is the very proud mother of an eight-and-one-half pound son, named Nickey. Mr. Frank Morovec is also proud. *The Star* is proud too."

"Nobody has ever been run over by a car in Valsetz, or knocked down either—by a car, we mean."

A group of Valsetz loggers pause beside their steam donkey engine on a spur rail line where logs were loaded onto flatcars for the ride to the mill. Picture taken around 1928. (Photo courtesy Jingles Lambert)

Valsetz planing mill workers pose for this group photo taken approximately 1940. (Photo courtesy Jingles Lambert)

"'Smudge,' is a she, we wish she were a he."

"Daddy says he will build his mountain lodge for tired business girls if Willkie gets elected."

"We have one subscriber named, 'Cake,' and one named, 'Cookey.'"

"The harvest moon shines over the Valsetz hills at night and it's very beautiful."

"A new subscriber, A Chinese girl, Sut Beak Lau, from Hilo, Hawaii, read about *The Star* in a Hawaiian newspaper."

"There is a new graveled road right thru town.
One ball player got married, and one got hurt.
Curtis had two teeth out, and everybody got a deer.
Anita has a new baby brother."

"And in our next issue we will be pleased to announce Wendell Willkie as our next President of the United States."

TOGETHER WE STAND
AUTUMN–NOVEMBER 1940

Folks in Valsetz had a certain camaraderie among them, a dedicated spirit of support that reflected an arm-in-arm stand seldom witnessed in large urban areas. Indiscernible in routine day-to-day activities, the esprit de corps became most evident through the community's backing of local school athletic events.

Residents of the community supported Valsetz teams with large turnouts for their games. The high school football team competed in the eight-man, Class "B" league. The boys' fortunes were not always commensurate with the undaunting enthusiasm and support provided by the townfolks. Dorothy Anne reported in a 1938 issue of *The Star*: "The Valsetz high football team lost to Perrydale 45 or 50 to nothing." Even the exact score was unimportant. What was important was the fact that nearly everyone in town attended to cheer for the Valsetz Cougars.

The motto of the final graduating class of 1984—last before the town's planned destruction—epitomized the sense of self-worth and team spirit of the Valsetz students.

"Only as high as I can reach can I grow,
Only as far as I seek can I go,
Only as deep as I look can I see,
Only as much as I dream can I be."

In 1928, the community recognized the need for a gymnasium for indoor winter sports. Once the decision to build was made, responsibility for various portions of the project was volunteered. Cobbs & Mitchell supplied the lumber, the millworkers furnished most of the labor and the loggers agreed to raise funds for whatever expenses would be incurred. The gymnasium was definitely a project by all the members of the community and reflected their total, dedicated town spirit.

*   *   *   *   *   *

Dorothy Anne's disappointment in the presidential election matched the despair of Republicans around the country.

"We have just received the most terrible blow of our career. We had everything planned that Wendell Willkie would be elected. Everything went wrong, and we could hardly stand it when people who voted for President Roosevelt began laughing and poking us."

"Franklin tried to look bold and courageous, but you could see it plain enough—we don't mean Franklin Roosevelt, we mean Franklin Thomas, the Assistant Editor of *The Star*.

We will finish the 7th grade, and then we don't know what our future will be on account of having to help pay the Debt."

"All the other newspapers will stand for unity with President Roosevlt, and we will join them, too. But we are still kind of mad."

"Mr. Chas. I. Pecker, of Lynn, Mass., said that 'Waddy,' the 80-year old elephant at Franklin Park Zoo, died on the very day Wendell Willkie was defeated."

"When first we heard the awful news, we almost thought we'd die. Please don't try to comfort us, go 'way and let us cry."

"This is Thanksgiving month and we give thanks for 21 million good strong firm Republicans and altho' we are sorry Daddy won't be able to build his mountain lodge for tired business girls, we are thankful he fixed our leaky roof at last."

"Mr. Thomas, our superintendent looked very pale on election eve at 9:30. Mr. Grout looked sad. Mr. McLean played checkers real fast. Mr. Harry Starr stayed awake all night. Mr. Roth, our principal, didn't eat. Walter Mitchell shivers on account of democracy.

And Daddy took a hot bath and shut the radio off."

"We have no policeman or sheriff in Valsetz, but nobody ever takes anything except once a man took a blanket but he brought it right back on account of not knowing it was his brother's."

"Mother had to put all the pictures of Wendell Willkie in the stove the next morning. She had tears in her eyes. She said it was like striking a match to democracy."

"Next month we will talk about Santa Claus."

"If any of our subscribers find any mistakes in our English please write us and let us know, on account of having so much trouble with our predicates in the 7th grade."

"At breakfast table we have so much fun. Mr. Richmond, our assistant professor who thinks kids should be spanked, and Mr. Webber, our timekeeper, who is a philosopher. Daddy talks the most but he doesnt' talk so much since Willkie wasn't elected."

"Grandma Hobson passed away in Salem last month. She was 83 and wanted to vote for Wendell Willkie."

"ADV. Our lumber is nice and smooth, you know, and hasn't any dents. Buy now and start to build, start building for defense."

"This morning we had a cup of chocolate and feel much better. Things look much brighter. We will begin to fight again and in 1944 we think Wendell Willkie will be President of the United States."

"Weather Forecast: Very Dark and Gloomy."

SUGARLOAF—VALSETZ POST OFFICES
AUTUMN–DECEMBER, 1940

In 1946 the U.S. Supreme Court upheld a U.S. Court of Claims decision which, in effect, reimbursed the Siletz, Yaquina, Neschisnis and Alsea descendants for land taken from them in 1865. The deal slipped through like osmosis. Much of the disputed acreage had been alloted to early settlers through the U.S. Homestead provisions. Many of those homesteads were gobbled up by individual speculators who sold out to large timber interests. The original Cobbs & Mitchell acreage was a conglomeration of smaller claims they purchased from a shrewd broker who had gathered up allotments totalling nearly 36,000 acres.

Stepping back in history 135 years, we would see startling differences on the steep Valsetz hillsides from then to the modern times of today. Back in those days, the Cascade range was relatively untouched, virgin old-growth timber grew thick as hair on a dog's back. Today, the monster trees are mostly gone, replaced by second and third-growth timber interspersed by clear-cut areas of grey stumps.

Fanno creek formed the drainage of Fanno ridge, so named by Oscar Fanno whose cabin stood at the little stream's juncture with the south fork of the Siletz river in 1894. The area of timbered hillsides was named Sugarloaf because of the shape of a nearby mountain ridge. Andrew Porter made the first known survey in 1894. The Sugarloaf post office was only a crude log cabin when it opened on April 16, 1895 with John S. Wright as the first postmaster. One can only surmise that lack of patronage forced closure of the post office on April 30, 1904.

It was to be sixteen years later that the Valsetz post office, in nearly the same location, was opened for business November 6, 1920. It remained in operation for sixty-four years, closing with the planned destruction of Valsetz itself in 1984.

* * * * * *

Dorothy Anne had this to report in *The Star*:
"Once again we are glad to say Merry Christmas to all our readers,

friends and subscribers, and peace on earth, good will to all the Democrats. We are feeling very kindly to everybody now on account of Xmas presents."

"We wish to announce that we are celebrating the birthday of *The Valsetz Star*, which is three years old this month. Yesterday we dug up one of our first copies and it certainly sounded silly.

Franklin says they still sound silly, but we have a great many subscribers—nearly 600—and people write us little letters about things.

One woman wrote to ask us if we could tell her anything about ground cherries and if they grew in the Northwest. We looked it up and they do. They look like small tomatoes, and grow on low bushes.

One woman from New York wanted to know do we really see many Indians in Oregon. And we answered, 'No we do not except the girls at Chemawa Indian School near Salem, who look like glamour girls.

A high school girl in St. Louis, Mo., wanted to know what in the world we do for amusement away off in the hills like this.

Well, we play baseball and have a Xmas Glee Club, and are selling fudge to buy a volley ball, and every night when the mail comes in we stand in the post office lobby and laugh and cackle something fierce.

A man in Cleveland, Ohio, wanted to know do we intend to become journalists. No, we do not, we are getting ready to fight for democracy as soon as we can."

"We stand firm and believe in the United States, and Cobbs & Mitchell, and the Republicans, and England and Wendell Willkie and Greece."

"We have just discovered that two of our oldest and nicest subscribers are Democrats. We couldn't believe it! They are Adeline Merriam Conner and her husband who live at 'The Cedars', in San

Juan, California. Adeline Merriam Conner is poet laureate of the lumber industry and is blind and very lovely. We have received many letters and poems from her.

She doesn't understand why people say such dreadful things about our presidents, from George Washington down. Below is a poem which she sent us last week. It is called, 'Just Wonderin.'"

"I wonder about presidents in this our freeborn nation, they come to serve us as they may, from every rank and station;
    And as each one accepts the post, to which our vote assigns him,
    The half of us exalt his name, the other half maligns him."

"We have received many letters since the election from people who wished to cheer us up. Several enclosed a dollar bill. We cheered up right away."

"ADV. Hurry up and phone your order, there's not much space this time.
    Get some Cobbs & Mitchell lumber, so many words won't rhyme."

"Jingles has been voted the most outstanding man of the year in Valsetz on account of catching so many muskrats in his traps."

"The day after Willkie was defeated, Mother changed all the furniture around in the living room—then sat down in a rocking chair and said she guessed things weren't so bad after all."

"Thanksgiving in Valsetz was a great success. Several people were sick."

"Al Lang ran over a deer on the mountain road and wrecked his car."

"'Nickey' Morovec was terribly disappointed in the election. All his ancestors are Republicans. He is one-month old."

"Mrs. Guy West came back to live in Valsetz, but the ladies won't ask for the silver dish back."

"Bill Mitchell went to Quantico, Va., to become a lieutenant in the Marines. He can't get married for two years. He doesn't care."

"There will be a big Xmas tree and school program Dec. 23rd, but Randy Butler won't be Santa Claus any more because all the kids know him now."

Oregon's First, Most, Biggest
Winter–January, 1941

Dorothy Anne's beloved state of Oregon was, "the new kid on the block" among other states in the U.S., coming into the Union in 1869. Although young by comparison, the Beaver State can lay claim to many important points of interest, happenings, and "firsts," among U.S. states.

Important to former Valsetz residents, the Douglas fir was honored as the Oregon State tree in 1939. In that same year, a distant relative of Dorothy's, Coach Howard Hobson, took the Oregon Ducks to the NCAA Division #1 basketball championships, and Northwest Airlines opened in Portland.

Among deepest—largest—greatest—, Oregon's Crater lake is the deepest lake in the U.S. at 1,932-feet. Hell's Gorge of the Snake river, on the Utah/Oregon border is the deepest river gorge in the country, measuring 7,900-feet. (Oregon can only claim half-a-deepest, sharing with Utah.) The mighty Columbia river is the largest river in the western hemisphere flowing to the Pacific Ocean. (Again, half-a-largest with Washington.)

Did you know that 25% of the nation's llamas are Oregon born and bred? Talking about animals, Oregon's Clatsop county first held an open season on elk in 1938. *"Gerber Legendary Blades,"* was founded in Portland in 1939, the same year TV commentator, Brent Musberger, was born in the Rose City.

Oregon's state motto is, "The Union," (whatever that means.)

Are they referring to the Teamster's; our country 'tis of thee; or Fergie's wedding?

The state flower is Oregon grape, bird is western meadowlark. The world's biggest log cabin was built in Portland for the 1905 Lewis and Clark Exposition. That can't be claimed anymore, it burned down. A record high temperature of 119-degrees was established for Oregon in 1938, at Pendleton. Oregon's record low was minus 54-degrees in 1933 at Seneca, which I'd never heard of before either, but it's south of John Day, near Malheur National Forest.

In 1941, Grand Coulee dam, the world's largest man-made structure at that time, called the eighth wonder of the world, was completed. It is 46-stories tall, twelve city blocks wide, required eight-years to complete, and a heck'uva lot of cement.

On January 20, 1939, Leroy McCarthy went into the Oregon record books, having the dubious distinction of being the first person executed in Oregon's new gas chamber. Reportedly, he killed a man during a $26.00 robbery. Prior to that, Oregon's historic method of execution had been by hanging.

During the WWII ship-building boom, more than 1,175 vessels were built in the Portland/Vancouver area, many by Henry J. Kaiser who introduced the assembly-line, mass production method of fabricating ships. He later gave up ship-building for auto production.

O.S.U. won the Rose Bowl in 1942, beating Duke, 20-16. And finally, Oregon was the first state to require a beverage container deposit in 1971.

*　　*　　*　　*　　*　　*

It was a new year for Dorothy, Franklin and the Valsetz *Star*:

"Happy New Year to all the world, and we will pray each night that some time this year of 1941 there will be peace again in the world. And that people in Europe can put down their machine guns and take up their plows and hammers and nails and try to build back again and maybe there will be joy in their hearts, and maybe Hitler will feel sad at night when he goes to bed because when he closes his eyes he will see burning buildings, and children crying and sad fathers looking for their families, and then he will have to get up and walk around, and if he can't find any peace maybe he will kneel down, and pray to God."

Cobbs & Mitchell's Shay loky #104, tuggin' big sticks 'cross the high trestle over Sunshine creek. The iron horse was built by Willamette Iron and Steel Co., Portland. It was one of five steam locomotives that were the work horses of the C & M woods operation. (Photo courtesy Jingles Lambert)

"December was the nicest month of all last year. On the 27th we went to Portland and were luncheon guests of the 'Portland City Club.' We all sat on a platform and our stomachs almost left us. Mr. Templeton, our publisher, talked about *The Star*, and he did not look scared, so we felt better. A whole sea of faces stared at us, and we wished we were back in Valsetz.

Then Dr. Raymond B. Walker who is President of the club, opened the meeting with a potato masher, and we laughed, and Don Sterling, of the 'Oregon Journal' who wasn't afraid, smiled. And Mr. George McKenzie, who was born in Scotland and isn't afraid of anything, smiled, and Arden X. Pangborn and Jack and Frankie laughed right out. From then on we didn't want to go home. We sat at small tables and had lunch and we didn't have to pay for it. Mother sat at a table a short distance away and was having a grand time except her bunion hurt, and she looked across some tables and saw Mr. C.L. Starr, who is our vice-president, and wondered if his vegetables had been put through the sieve. But then she said nothing was ever perfect anyway."

"We spent the night at the home of our publisher, Mr. Templeton, who is a lumberman, but can play the violin swell. He played 'The Missouri Waltz,' and 'Blue Danube.' Hall Templeton played the recorder. Franklin sang, and George McKenzie played 'The Blue Bells of Scotland.' Mother sat in front of the fireplace and said she could almost see the Scottish moors, but she has never been there."

"And on down to the 'Equitable Savings & Loan Association' banquet at the 'Benson Hotel' where we were guests of Ralph Cake, who is president of the association. He is also Republican National Committeeman. Portland's Mayor Carson sat right close and made a speech. He is a Democrat, but not a New Dealer.

We felt better."

"Tommy Luke was there and he would like to know why he has never been mentioned in *The Valsetz Star*. He sells flowers down on the corner of Sixth and Alder, and when he shakes hands he almost cracks your bones."

"Mr. Ralph Cake is almost as nice as Mr. Templeton, and invited us out to his home for dinner. He has six trains upstairs, one bank downtown, three cars, two children, one maid, one wife, and a lot of camping equipment."

Down at the '*Oregon Journal*' office everybody was writing on a typewriter and running around with a piece of paper. Everyone there was so nice to us, but it's much easier to think sitting at our own card table."

"On Monday noon we were guests of the Herbert Templetons at a luncheon at '*The University Club*,' and there we met Mr. and Mrs. Cornwall. Mr. Cornwall is publisher of '*The Timberman*,' a magazine, and they are very good friends of the Claude McLeans of Valsetz. Mr. McLean is our logging superintendent."

"And most important of all was Nan Brewster, who writes, '*Faces and Places*,' for the '*Sunday Oregonian*.' She is very clever, but there is a terrible thing in her life. She can't get her husband to sit down when he carves!"

"Then came the last evening with The Broadcast, and by that time we weren't afraid of anything. Mr. Templeton got right up and told everybody just what he thought right thru the microphone."

"Thanks to Mr. Robert Thomas. Thanks to Mr. Harry Burton. Thanks to Joseph Sampietro. Thanks to '*Northwestern Neighbors*,' and

'KOIN.' Thanks to everybody who helped us to have such a perfect week in Portland."

"We received a letter from Mr. C.E. Fuge, of Oregon City, who is 77-years old. And he said, "On the night of your broadcast was I listening? I'll say I was, and when you sang 'The Swanee River,' I sang right along with you."

"It was very quiet in Valsetz on New Year's Eve. Everybody was awakened at midnight by the mill whistle blowing, but they just went right back to sleep again."

"We are sure President Roosevelt will guide us along the right way."

"Our foreign policy is to help a lot, mind our own business a little, and keep on taking vitamins."

"Weather forecast: Rains, but very gentle."

THE GREAT DEPRESSION
WINTER–FEBRUARY, 1941

When the 1930's Depression hit the U.S., people living in the Northwest fared significantly better than residents from other sections of America, especially city-dwellers. Like native Indians who had always subsisted totally from the land, Valsetzians had only to look around to see many opportunities for self-sustenance.

Following the great stockmarket crash, production in nearly every industry far outstripped demand. Lumber was no exception. At first, timbermen tried to curtail output to match sales. Along came the

New Deal's N.R.A. program which mandated production levels. As with most other federally-controlled market systems, it was unworkable and soon was declared unconstitutional by the U.S. Supreme Court. Uncontrolled free-wheeling supply and demand was found to be the most successful approach to levelling production.

The Civilian Conservation Corps. (C.C.C.) was the first federal program designed to offer economic relief that had a positive impact on Western Oregon. The public works program was offered to young men across the country and operated similar to a peacetime army. The "CCC" boys lived in camps, often tents, where they ate and slept, then worked building forest roads, trails, park projects, fire suppression on county, state and federal forestlands. They received a minimal wage from the federal government. A CCC camp was soon established in the Valsetz area.

The W.P.A. was another New Deal relief program established by President FDR during the Depression. It was also a public works program designed to provide a minimal wage to unemployed workers and assigned them to various public projects. Building Oregon's coast highway and bridges was one of the largest PNW jobs during the Depression.

As happened with most Oregon sawmills during the lean years, Valsetz loggers and millworkers experienced layoffs and production curtailments during the Depression. When Cobbs & Mitchell closed down early in the 1930's due to declining sales, there was 30-million board feet of lumber in the yard.

Many Northwesterners turned to Mother Nature's bounty to eke out a meager existence. Peeling cascara (chittum) bark, gathering ferns, fronds, and huckleberry brush for floral wholesalers, or picking blackberries were just a few optional avocations available. During Depression days, fern cutters were averaging two-cents for a bundle of 55 sword ferns. A person could snip around a hundred bundles a day, netting two dollars.

With meat, fish and berries from the forest, home-grown vegetables, eggs from a few chickens, the primary store-bought necessities were flour, salt and sugar. Coffee, even sugar, were considered luxuries.

During the Depression prices dropped almost forty-percent, food took an even larger decline. With dollars in short supply, bartering became a way of life for some. A person could wash dishes in a restaurant (if he could find one still in business) for a couple of hours in exchange for a meal.

Hard times continued even through 1938. Then, lumber orders began to increase with the European hostilities, and later sky-rocketed as WWII escalated. Valsetz and the nation were then back on a solid, though unfortunately war-time, economic footing.

*   *   *   *   *   *

The Valsetz Star weather forecast: "Many more inches of rain will fall."

"Special Editor's Note: Just three weeks before Wendell Willkie hopped off for England he sent us a letter which stirred us all over. We are printing it here so all of our readers will be stirred too. It was written at 109 East 42nd St., New York City, and read as follows:

'Dear Dorothy: Your earnest efforts in my behalf and the splendid work your newspaper accomplished have been brought to my attention. I want you to know that I am sincerely grateful.'

'Now that I am a private citizen again, I can only work shoulder to shoulder with you and every loyal American to preserve our democratic way of life, and it is heartening to know that in Valsetz, the principles for which I stand were so well upheld by you and your associates. Thank you again for your loyal support.'

Sincerely, (signed) Wendell L. Willkie."

"We have always been very fond of Wendell Willkie and we think he was very brave in saying what he thought. We think he is brave in 1941 when he tries to help all he can, and we are very glad that he doesn't stand in a corner and cry because he wasn't elected. We like him like we did."

"We have swung right into line behind President Roosevelt to help defend our country. We think he needs some good Republicans to help out. We will fight or sacrifice or starve in the daytime, and pray at night. We pray quite a lot anyway."

"We'll not talk about politics much this year, but don't think we aren't still Republicans."

"After reading several letters written to us we've about decided not to be a lawyer. One man wrote, 'Women are failures as lawyers. They lack nerve and are too soft.' And even one woman wrote from Chicago, 'Women talk too much, honey. Try something else.'

One lovely old man from Denver, who must be like Don Quixote, wrote that women should - 'Sit on a cushion, and sew a fine seam, and feed upon strawberries, sugar and cream.'

Then from a very smart young man in New York who signed his name with a great dash: 'Women? Huh, they make me sick. Law! That's a laugh. They better look after a man's stomach instead of his lawsuits.'

We've gotten quite discouraged over all this, and altho we can't see anything very interesting about stomachs we think maybe we had better just keep house. We hope the *Portland City Club* won't mind."

"We read an article in *"The Portland Oregonian,"* called, *"The Flag is Always There."* We read it twice. We hope everyone read it. After reading it we watched people in Valsetz. One night three loggers scurrying into supper glanced at the flag waving high in the park. They looked pleased. Two sawmill men noticed it. They passed us whistling. Some handle factory men glanced at the flag, and one said, "Great country, isn't it?'

We hope our flag will always proudly wave over Valsetz and the rest of the United States."

"We stand for the lend-lease aid to Britain, but we won't stand for everything."

(Things more local) "The third week in January we had 10.1 inches of rainfall and 4.5 inches fell one night. We are very proud of our rainfall. Everyone has large feet and nice complexions."

"Nobody in the east can find Valsetz on the map. Will somebody please do something about it?"

"It's time to renew your 1941 subscriptions if our readers don't mind."

"Jingles has several girls now on account of having caught enough mink in his traps to make a small fur coat. He is the outdoor type and has hair on his chest in the summer in the lumber yard."

"The ladies of the bridge club held their annual party for the husbands last month. The ladies all wore their best dresses, their fur coats, red fingernails, and large earrings. The men wore whatever they had."

"Daddy said the only time Hitler will kneel down and pray to God is when somebody knocks him down."

"Eugene Euwer, of Parkdale, Oregon said after seeing one or two issues of *The Star* he considered it just as important as the cat."

"Mr. Templeton, our publisher in Portland, and Mrs. Templeton spent a day in Valsetz on the 10th. They will leave soon for two weeks' vacation in California, where our publisher can rest and sleep in the sun. He hasn't slept since the broadcast in December."

"Don't forget your order this morning for Cobbs & Mitchell's nice smooth lumber."

THE VALSETZ COOKSTOVE
WINTER–MARCH, 1941

A typical Valsetz family home in winter.

The *"Watkins"* calendar hung by a nail on the barewood kitchen wall, the year, 1941. Mother x'ed out the days Father worked so she could guesstimate that month's paycheck.

The family's focal point was the black cookstove, from where life revolved. Its iron handle was used to pick up the flat, round stove lids, removable for shoving in another chunk of pungent, split fire wood. The monstrous singing teakettle emitted steam from its stubby spout. Criss-crossed wire or rope clotheslines were strung from wall-to-wall around the cookstove for drying rain-dampened pants and jackets, laundry, caps, hats and mittens. Sizzling water droplets disappeared in a puff of steam when dripped onto the hot stove. The curly-wire handle on the blue-black stove pipe adjusted the flu, as did the sliding iron handle on the stove's rear surface. The largest pans Mother owned were filled with water and set on the stove for Saturday night baths. When hot, the water was poured into the large, round galvanized wash tub that sat on the kitchen floor for the lucky first kid's bath. Murky, lukewarm water awaited kids number two, three or four. Mother and Father bathed after the kids went to bed.

The large, round tub did double-duty. On laundry day Mother filled it with warm water and dirty clothes, then put the two wooden legs of her crinkly, ridged washboard into the tub. Applying strong, brown Fels Naptha soap and a ton of rub-a-dub-dub got the clothes clean. The gray wash was rinsed, and during nice weather hung outside on wire clotheslines to dry. On the other 360 days of the year, Mother's laundry was dried on the back porch or above the very versatile cookstove.

Beneath and alongside the kitchen stove was an array of damp shoes and boots. Father's caulked work boots were given preference, but not too close to the heat. When the stove was loaded with pitchy, dry wood, dampers opened, it glowed cherry red like a neon ace of hearts in the darkened kitchen. With modernization came the tall, shiny cylindrical hot water tank attached to the rear of the stove. No gauges, Mother felt the top of the tank with her work-wrinkled hand to determine the amount of hot water it held.

And, my oh my, the delicious delicacies Mother concocted from that stove's oven—truly a miracle black box. The oven's temperature gauge was Mother's hand, thrust into the oven and only satisfied when it felt, "just right." Probably more accurate than today's digitals. The oven's controls were either more, or less wood, or opening the oven door, or deftly manipulating the damper.

On Thanksgiving Mother could roast a twenty-pound bird, bake three pies and do a pan of sweet spuds, all browned to a Martha Stewart approved goldish hue. The only downside was the kitchen temperature zooming higher than the melting point of titanium. At that time the only relief was opening the kitchen door and warming up outdoors Valsetz.

*　*　*　*　*　*

The Valsetz Star weather forecast: "Sunshine and more sunshine."

"Special Editor's Note: Sometimes The *Portland Oregonian* writes a whole editorial about an old gray cat, or the first spring trillium, so today we thought we would write about the meadowlark we heard in our back yard—we have no front yard—and the lacy white flowers of the spirea bush making a foamy spray like the Pacific Ocean which is only fifteen miles down the canyon but you have to go around until the CCC boys get the shortcut finished.

And the pussy willows in the blue vase, and Doctor Spray's new eggshell Chrysler upholstered in maroon with a piano in it, and Mrs. Heydon's new between Eleanor and Soldier blue coat, and Franklin—not President Roosevelt—but Franklin the Assistant Editor of *The Star*, selling any old thing he can to get money to buy marbles with, and Mother shuddering on account of 'Out of the Night,' by 'The-Book-Of-The-Month,' and then looking at the yellow primroses and feeling sad and 'lifted' again, and that our world is good and the flag still waves high in the park, and oh, yes, will the editor of the 'Portland Oregonian,' please look away back and find the copy with the editorial, 'The Flag is Always There,' and send it to one of our subscribers, Mrs. Thelma E. Conydon, 720 Ft. Washington Ave., New York, N.Y. She said in her letter, 'Will you tell me where to get a copy of 'The Oregonian' with the article, 'The Flag is Always There.' I liked what you said about it, it brought back the same feeling I had about the flag on Washington's birthday in Fort Tryon Park high above the Hudson.'"

"My! This is the longest editorial we have ever written."

"Franklin doesn't think Japan will attack us on account of all the cactus plants in the public market, and we think Mussolini looks so silly all puffed out, and he yelled so in our living room a year ago, and now he hasn't done anything and Hitler yells so loud too, and we can't understand what he says, and we think maybe he is a little afraid too, like the time we chewed our gum so fast when we got pushed near the edge of the cliff high on the mountain road."

"We are very sad today. We have just learned thru one of our subscribers, Mr. C.G. Bird, Manager of the 'Stockton Lumber Company,' of Stockton, California, that one of our oldest subscribers, Mr. Frank W. Trower, a San Francisco lumberman, and past president of the 'International Hoo Hoo Club,' has passed away. Just a week ago we received a letter from him. Twice a month he wrote us a long letter of five or six pages, and sent us pictures, clippings, and poems. He was a strong Republican and hoped that *The Star* would live forever. He also introduced us by letter to Adelaide Merriam Conner, blind poet laureate of the lumber industry."

Dorothy Anne Hobson is pictured on the arm of her father, Henry Hobson, on the day of her marriage to Frederick Graham, August 20, 1949. (Photo courtesy Graham family)

"We feel like we know our subscribers, altho we have never seen many of them. We wonder about each one, and do they like movies, and ice cream, and Wendell Willkie?"

"Franklin and the editor like America because we can put butter an inch thick on a big heel of hot bread after school."

"ADV. Spring is here. Order a pile of Cobbs & Mitchell nice smooth lumber, and start building something."

"Bert Yeager, an editor, of Toronto, Canada, wants to insert an ad in *The Star* next month inviting excursionists to visit Canada this summer.
We will not charge him anything for the ad on account of the United States liking Canada and England so well."

"Lloyd R. Smith, Corporation Commissioner for the State of Oregon, wrote us that *'Time Magazine,'* and *The Valsetz Star* were the only two periodicals he cared anything about."

"Spring came to Valsetz early this year. Three babies were born, one boy broke his arm, one cut his head open. The Valsetz ladies hemmed a thousand diapers for the *'Red Cross.'*

Four batches of kittens were born under our house. Fred Shaad's housekeeper left, and Mrs. Thomas set the first hen."

"Mrs. Roosevelt said for the American women to tighten up their belts, but Mother said she could hardly breathe now when she gets her new corsets on."

"Dan Usher was drafted and will soon leave to join the army and fight for Valsetz and the rest of the United States. We are sacrificing something fierce now."

"The Parent Teachers had a white elephant sale and nobody knew what was in the packages. They had Bill Carver auction them off, and my, how he can make money. He made everything sound so good, and Mother paid two dollars for two tiny gold fish. She thought she was getting a lace table cloth. Before the evening was over everybody was in debt, but they cleared a pile of money for library books."

BACK THEN IN VALSETZ
SPRING–APRIL, 1941

During winter, the roiling dark clouds were so low it seemed we could reach and touch them if we stood on Mother's wooden kitchen chair, the one with the broken lattice back. The sun was hidden for days, maybe weeks we didn't see it. We knew it was up there some-where, shining on someone else, or was it?

The living room window was forever dimpled with sparkly rain-drop buttons in a bumpy pattern. The dog was always wet, and the mud, my goodness, the mud was everywhere. A bootjack was kept outside the kitchen door for easy taking off our boots, and a mud-scraper was always kept handy for cleaning footware.

The kitchen floor was yellow linoleum, criss-crossed with squiggly brown circles looked like mushrooms that had come up after a hard rain. Mother scrubbed off the mud we tracked in with a wooden-handled clamp rag mop.

On nice days we left the kitchen door open and our wooden screen door kept the flies and mosquitos out. Those mosquitos, Daddy said he saw two of them carrying off a logger while a third one went back after his cross-cut saw. But our screen door was kept good and tight by a long spring in the middle.

Before ice-boxes we had a screen-covered cooler just outside the kitchen door, near the woodpile. It got cold enough at night most things in the cooler kept pretty good. But in the middle of summer, daddy sunk a barrel in a pond and we kept our cool things in there.

When the laundry had dried, Mother ironed the important clothes with two flat irons she kept on the stove to get hot. She'd use one while the other one was heating, then trade off. My play clothes didn't get ironed, neither did Daddy's outdoor pants. But she carefully ironed my crinoline party dress, her one fancy chemise, and Daddy's dress-up shirts and pants.

It wasn't very far to the Cobbs & Mitchell store run by Mr. Grout. But then, nothing was very far away in Valsetz. We got most of our supplies from the store in Falls City, but sometimes Mother would run out and she'd send me to get something from Mr. Grout. That was always fun walking the plank streets and sidewalk, trying to miss all the mud puddles and keep my patent leather shoes clean.

Mr. Grout's store was a wondrous place to visit. Reading the many different labels on the cans and jars could take hours but after awhile, he'd ask, "Is there something I can help you find?" Then I knew it was time to leave. Most of the food stuff came from right here in Oregon. But once I found a label that came all the way from New York City.

I've heard Daddy say, "It's a small world sometimes." I guess he's sure right about that.

*   *   *   *   *   *

The April edition of the *Valsetz Star* had its longest weather forecast yet: "April showers, northerly off-the- mountain winds, some hail, light frost, but it will all be gone before we get up."

"Special Editor's Note: We were going to write an article on the Balkan situation but everything happens so fast that we are afraid the situation would be over before we could get the copy in to our publisher.

We admire young King Peter, and our hearts went right along with him when he rode down the street on his white horse and tried to look so brave, and maybe he was a little scared too, but he has spirit

166

and millions of his people are helping keep Yugoslavia independent.

We hope they will fight like we would fight in this country if anybody came after us. We are just waiting for Hitler to come after us—Franklin, not Franklin Roosevelt, but the assistant editor—is all ready to spring.

We are taking a new kind of vitamin. It has three letters in it and you feel just terribly militant all at once."

"We are moving our office because everything looks serious and we only have tar on our roof and everybody says the Panzer troops stop at nothing. Two people wrote us that the world will come to an end in May. But we hope not because life is so much fun and we just got a new shade of red for our fingernails. And then Matsuoka, the Japanese Foreign Minister, had a cup of tea with Hitler, and Russia and Japan had a meeting and whispered and then laughed until they shook. And James Roosevelt got married again and so did Ralph Hurst, one of our loggers. But we just nearly died when Jack Benny's hen laid an egg over the radio in a drugstore just in time for his malted milk."

"Last month we received the following letter from Herbert Hoover. We are very proud to have a letter from Herbert Hoover. Once before he dropped us a line. 'The Waldorf-Astoria, New York, N.Y., March 14, 1941. My dear Dorothy Anne: At various times during the last couple of years I have seen copies of your paper, 'The Valsetz Star,' and I want you to know I have enjoyed reading them. I am in hopes you will continue to keep up your good work. Yours faithfully, (signed) Herbert Hoover.'"

"Merriam Conner, the blind poet laureate, was the winner of the first honorable mention for her poem, 'Worrying Worm,' from more than 800 entries from all over the U.S. and several foreign countries.

We wish we could copy the poem here, but the poor worm had so many worries it would take up all the page. He feared the birds and the garden toad, the hoe and the rake, human feet, and the fearsome hen. And then he turned into a butterfly and was afraid of the rain and only in the last few lines did he find any happiness....'Of all the things I have dreaded, said he, Not a single one ever happened to me.'"

"ADV. Don't look around and waste your time,
And think that you might save a dime.
Just buy the best you can get,
It's Cobbs & Mitchell's, you just bet."

"Local and Personal: The editor will have to be in Salem for awhile on account of her nose, but will come back quite often to answer letters and keep in touch with our subscribers, and Mother said she would save all the gossip."

This one-lane gravel road leads to the now obliterated Valsetz townsite. The Boise-Cascade Co. allows no trespassing through yellow gate. (Author photo)

"Lloyd Smith, Corporation Commissioner, would like very much to have Mr. Starr, our vice-president, invite them all to Valsetz again this year for dinner, but he does not like to say too much about it."

"We had a late Sunday night supper, and had scrambled eggs like Mrs. Roosevelt's.

Mr. H.P. Lee, one of our subscribers in Portland, says, 'The Valsetz Star comes to me like a bracing wholesome breeze from your fragrant forests.' Isn't that pretty? He is a democrat too, but has always been very fond of us."

"Daddy is hunting a good location to build his lodge for tired business girls."

"Jingles will be married very soon. He is terribly in love with Maxine. He hurried to Portland to buy a ring and was going to pay a hundred dollars for it, but when he got there he was so thrilled and excited he paid two hundred dollars for it."

"Mrs. Grout is the best dressed woman in Valsetz.

Mrs. Starr makes the best chiffon pie.

Mrs. Frazer is the best bridge player."

"We think Hitler will get licked but we don't know when."

"Important men who wear bow ties: George McKenzie, Bert Thomas, Hall Templeton, Bing Crosby, Allen Cleveland, President Roosevelt, and Hank."

"We received a copy of 'Don Quixote,' autographed by Nina Fedorova who received ten thousand dollars for writing, 'The Family.'"

"Last Saturday, 12th, was the opening day of fishing season and everyone came in from the pond with big baskets of fish."

JINGLES III
SPRING–MAY, 1941

Born in Sweden in 1909, Ingvar, "Jingles" Lambert celebrated his ninetieth birthday with family on Thanksgiving Day, 1999. Originally, his dad and the kids "bummed around" Canada for a few years, landing in Valsetz in 1922.

"Cobbs & Mitchell were going full blast in those days," Ingvar recalled. "They had over 500 men working in the woods and the sawmill, putting in ten-hour shifts. The mill was sawin' over 300,000 feet of lumber each day."

When asked what a thirteen-year old did for excitement in a lumber town back in those days, Lambert replied, "We attended school, always had our chores, and beyond that, the woods was our playground." Then with a boyish grin, he remembered, "Oh yes, we weren't supposed to, but when nobody was looking, we'd sneak off and walk the logs in the millpond. The ones with bark were easy enough but in some places the bark had been knocked off and those logs were kind of slippery. Some of us took an unplanned swim. It didn't bother us none, livin' in Valsetz we were often wet anyway."

Lambert recalled he was one of about seventy kids in the Valsetz school. "I went to school through the eighth grade, then quit to begin working in the woods," he said. "I did just about everything, tried to learn as many jobs as I could. But my favorite was highclimbing," he told me.

"Back in those days we didn't have any of those portable spar trees. We had to climb a good lookin' tree, top it and then rig it for yarding logs to the cold deck or loading site. Climbing with spurs was kinda dangerous but I was always careful and never had any serious accidents. Some of those spar trees were 200-feet tall. The biggest danger was having the tree split when you topped it. You're hangin' up there by your belt and if the tree split it could crush you. After sawing the top off and it fell, you'd always get a good ride. The tree could sway back and forth more than twenty-feet. That was the fun part," he said, as an impish grin spread across his large-featured face.

"Cobbs & Mitchell closed down for awhile during the Depression," Jingles recalled. "I was brought back to the logging side in 1934. I'd been falling and bucking timber and got pretty good at it. I remember once they had a special order for navy spars and they asked me to bring them in. The trees had to be near perfect, yellow Doug fir, 68-feet long with minimum diameters of 44-inches. If not felled properly, they would get cracked or busted up."

Once he selected the high-grade tree, Ingvar said he would fall several other trees to accumulate a big pile of boughs. "I would make a thick bed of those boughs exactly where I planned to fall the spar tree. Next, I had to make sure the spar wouldn't hit any stumps when it landed. Stumps can really mess up a tree if it hits one. Then, all I had to do was make certain I fell the tree onto my cushioned bed," he concluded.

Listening to "Jingles," he made it sound so easy.

In *The Valsetz Star*, Dorothy Anne reported: "We have started this month to help our country. We bought two government savings stamps and stopped putting so much butter on our bread."

"We have just received some very exciting last minute news. We will leave Portland by airplane with our publisher, Mr. Templeton, on Monday, May 19th for Los Angeles, to be guests of 'We, The People,' over C.B.S. on Tuesday, May 20th. Mother will go too, but she is awfully scared about the airplane."

"A long time ago in our second or third issue of *The Star*, we said we stood for Peace. Well, some people get terribly mad if we talk about peace now and they call us 'Appeasers,' and one boy called us much worse than that, and so we have changed some, but not much, and we think maybe we could ride along beside the ships to England to visit and we wouldn't make anybody mad. We don't want to make anybody mad now, anyway, on account of being guests of *The Portland Rose Festival* next month."

"Everyone is badly upset, and things are in an awful mess,
    Can some of our readers please guess, what's all the fuss over Hess?"

"Judith Waller, Director of Public Service and Education of '*The National Broadcasting Company*,' of Chicago, is one of our subscribers, and has just been named one of the 53 outstanding women of America on account of making so many strides in 50 years."

"Mr. Worth W. Preston, a real estate broker of Los Angeles, enjoys the 'piquancy and flavor,' of *The Star*, but he would like to know what 'financial jugglery' we use to expand a 2¢ per month publication into a dollar per year subscription. Well, we don't know—we just send out a copy of *The Star* and say it's a dollar a year by mail and our subscribers send us a dollar and nobody says anything."

"We wish President Roosevelt would tell us how to sacrifice so we could help our country more, but we do not want to give up ice cream."

"Mrs. Roosevelt said, 'This isn't going to be a nice quiet comfortable world,' but we don't care much, because we don't like to be nice and quiet anyway."

Pictured from the gravel road junction to the former Valsetz townsite. Stands of green timber are interspersed with logged-off hillsides in the Boise-Cascade Valsetz tree farm. (Author photo)

"Hess dropped into Scotland and eggs are going up."

"Mrs. Roosevelt said in Portland, 'A great many things in this country have to be set right.' We have started to clean up our yard."

"Jingles will be married to Maxine on Sunday, June 15th, just over the hill in Dallas. All his life he has been hunting for Maxine. She keeps books and is very dainty. Jingles is very strong and tall and blonde and was almost born in Valsetz. He can pile lumber faster than anybody and is terribly anxious to settle down and have a green lawn."

"Tom Allen subscribed to *The Star* for ten years."

"We wish we could have a big party at Valsetz and invite all our subscribers and have ice cream."

"Mrs. Grout and Mrs. Thomas are on a reducing diet. Mrs. Grout lost five pounds, then gained two. Mrs. Thomas lost two pounds, then gained one. Then Mrs. Grout gained another, then lost. If Mrs. Grout loses two pounds next week she will be the same as Mrs. Thomas was last week."

"We are thrilled over being guests next month of *The Portland Rose Festival*. We have a special invitation from Mr. Chester Moores who is president of the *Rose Show*, and Mr. J.O. Fisher, distributor of the Dodge and Plymouth cars in Portland, has tendered the use of a decorated automobile for us while we are there. Mother is terribly excited and is airing everything on the line and has sent for a new bottle of gas tablets."

"Getting your nose fixed isn't so much fun, but Dr. Finley, nose specialist in Salem, is wonderful, only at the hospital there was such excitement—on one side a man died, and on the other side a baby was born, but we got six new subscribers to *The Star*."

"Weather forecast: Buckets of rain lately, but it will clear in a few weeks."

"ADV. Call up and buy some lumber. It's nice and smooth, and keen, and the price, we want to tell you, is the best you've ever seen. From Cobbs & Mitchell, natcherly!!"

EXCITING TIMES
SPRING–JUNE, 1941

Dorothy Anne Hobson, inspired editor that she was, wrote that her June, 1941 issue was a "Special Deluxe Edition."

The mid-year Valsetz *Star* carried stories about two exciting experiences the young lady had enjoyed, while making recommendations on, "How seventh and eighth-graders should act when in love, and some style hints."

"We hope our readers will read our Special June Edition from cover to cover and then pass it along to their neighbors and please, will you all try our fudge recipe.

It is the best you have ever tasted and be sure and let it cool before beating, until it's just about as warm as our subscriber's hearts which is just right.

And now for our thrilling trip to Hollywood and our talk over the air on 'We The People,' program on May, 20th. We left Portland by airplane on Monday, May 19th, with our publisher, Mr. Herbert Templeton, who looked after everything for us.

Mother was terribly scared at first and gripped the sides of the plane, but then she thought of Mrs. Roosevelt and sat right up and enjoyed the trip.

Someone asked us what was the most outstanding thing on our trip. We think it was the gum. Every half-hour the stewardess passed around gum on account of our ears cracking and by the time we got to Hollywood we had the swellest big wad!

At Hollywood we met Mr. Carroll O'Meara, manager of *Young and Rubicam Advertising Co.*, who had charge of our part on, 'We The People,' program and was so nice to us. He was our host at a steak dinner and brought 'Amos,' of 'Amos and Andy,' over to our table so we could meet him. The steaks cost two dollars and a quarter each—

Mother took a peek at the price when nobody was looking—but when 'Amos' came over to our table she got so excited she forgot to eat her steak.

Another terrible thrill we had was when Mr. O'Meara took us to *Paramount Studios*. We had to pass three policemen to get inside but Mr. O'Meara walked right past them. Once inside, we met Mr. Jack Gershberg who is very handsome. At first we thought he was a movie star but he is a publicity agent. He went with us inside the Movie Restaurant for lunch and told us the names of all the stars. They were all smiling and eating ice cream just like we were. My! We will never forget it.

When we left there we drove past Mae West's apartment and Mr. Templeton wanted to get out.

On Wednesday night, May 21st, we drove to Pasadena for dinner at Mary Patterson Routt's home. She is a writer and friend of our publishers. There we met Carrie Jacobs Bond, who wrote, 'The End of A Perfect Day.' Carrie Jacobs Bond is eighty years old, and at the dinner she told us about the first time she went to sing at the White House. She was quite young and poor then, and while she waited in the lobby for the President to appear, she wished she hadn't come. She felt so lonely and poor and out of place, her dress was shabby and her sleeves were too short, and her hat wasn't right. Just then she glanced up and right behind her was a picture of Abraham Lincoln. He was gazing down at her.

Suddenly everything seemed all right. Her heart lifted and she crossed the lobby and sang for the President.

Mother whisked a tear away real fast."

"Everyone was swell to us at the 'Columbia Broadcasting Station.' Everything went fine on the broadcast except we almost had the hiccoughs, and Mary Astor swept right past us in the lobby of the broadcasting station. Nobody in California ever heard of Valsetz. Some of them never even heard of Portland."

"We would like to thank Mr. Gabriel Heatter of 'We The People,' program in New York for inviting us to be his guest on the air. We will send him a year's subscription to *The Star*, but we don't know what else to do."

"We had another extra special nice thing happen to us this month. We were guests of the *Portland Rose Festival* for four days and stayed at the *Mallory Hotel*.

Mr. Chester Moores, president of the *Rose Festival* told us that it cost forty thousand dollars to put on the show, and Mother didn't order anything expensive at the hotel for fear they might go broke like we do here sometimes.

Everything was made of roses and the bands were playing and the queen was smiling and every place we went we had ice cream with frozen roses on top. And always at the luncheons they served dainty lamb chops with pale blue frills on.

Mr. Joe Fisher and Mr. Jueneman, our escorts, took us every place in a long cream-colored Dodge car decorated in pink and orchid flowers.

Tommy Luke gave Mother a huge armful of red roses to carry in the parade, and when the bands began to play and the people were clapping, Mother thought she was the queen and was bowing but they were clapping for the Governor.

Daddy couldn't come because of his arches and besides he is worried about taxes.

Two terrible things happened—it almost rained Wednesday night when they were ready to crown the queen, and Mother lost her gas tablets on 6th and Washington Streets."

"Thank you, Mr. Moores, Mr. Ireland, Art Kirkham, Joe Fisher,

Fred Jueneman and others, for one of the happiest times we have ever had."

"Everybody in Valsetz is one hundred per cent American and if anybody attacks us we will all fight until the last ditch in the mountain road is gone."

"Jingles was married last Sunday at two o'clock and turned perfectly white."

"Mrs. Brown of Bandon, Oregon, would like to hear some news about her friends the Ted Holems, who run a dairy down below Valsetz.
Well, they are getting along fine and have several new calves."

"Franklin, not Franklin Roosevelt, but Franklin Thomas, the Assistant Editor of *The Star*, thinks the international situation is getting fierce but he doesn't want to give up movies."

"The Valsetz Baseball Club has won every game this season. Last Sunday was a double header at Mack's Field near Falls City and three hundred people yelled wildly when 'Gibby' reached slowly into the air with one hand and picked off a ball which was roaring over the fence. In the first game he made a home run and Mr. Thomas ran out on the field and gave him a dollar. He will take it to the Army with him."

"Franklin, the Assistant Editor, received a pair of carrier pigeons. He is getting a message ready to send to Hitler."

"Mrs. Ebbert, our fourth grade teacher, left real fast for Bremerton, Washington, where her husband makes twenty dollars a day."

"Advice to Seventh and Eighth Grade girls who might be falling in love:

Do not act like you are crazy about the boys even if you are.

Keep up on the baseball scores, but don't act like you know too much—eighth grade boys can't bear it.

Mention how tall and strong he is but don't mention his big ears.

Try to act dainty and small even if you aren't.

Don't eat too many weinies even if you want several more.

Don't be too serious and don't laugh too much. Don't talk too much. Don't be silly, don't be too sensible.

Don't act loud, don't pose, don't tell the boys exactly what you think; don't act dumb, but don't act too smart either.

Let them help you with your arithmetic even if you have it all figured out before.

If you do all of these, maybe you will get a chance to wear your formal."

"Table Manners: Never mop the gravy off your plate with a hunk of bread—but it sure tastes good.

Never lick your ice cream dish. Leave a little there if you can, but it's terribly hard to do."

"ADV. Go to Canada to spend your vacation this summer. Don't go to Europe, you'll get hit with something.

Canada will welcome you and won't hit you and won't charge you too much."

Dorothy Anne's Suggestions to Girls Regarding Boys:

"If you tie a large bow under your chin you will get several glances."

"When your boy friend brings you home in the evening, if it is after eight o'clock don't let him in—it is dangerous."

"Do not cuddle up too close to your boy friend—he will turn cold."

"Franklin, not Franklin Roosevelt, but Franklin the Assistant Editor of *The Star*, out for his daily stroll. He doesn't like bold girls."

"If some strange boy tries to date you just swish right past him."

"Wear neat aprons in the kitchen. Mop the floor every day if you think of it. Don't let the puppy stay in the kitchen too long."

KEEPING BUSY
SUMMER–JULY, 1941

Maxine Lambert recalls when she and "Jingles" were married, June 15, 1941. "Yes, payday," Ingvar laughed.

"Jing was thirty-one, I was twenty-one," she reminisced. "For the first few months we lived in an apartment in Dallas, then moved into a company house in Valsetz. At first it was very traumatic, I'd always lived in town, had never experienced isolation like Valsetz before. It was a totally different lifestyle but I soon became accustomed to it. Valsetz kind of grew on you, I liked it, in fact I'd do it all over again. People were so friendly, so supportive of one another. I spent a lot of time slunched over the back fence, jabbering with my neighbor, and that was alright," she mused.

Pert and petite Mrs. Lambert kept busy during the fifteen years she and "Jingles" lived in the wettest spot in Oregon. "I worked in the Valsetz lumber office awhile for Herbert Templeton," she remembered with a smile. "I clerked at the school, even worked as a waitress for a while in the Valsetz rec hall. Templetons were good friends, even attended our wedding. I was Valsetz correspondent for the Dallas and Salem papers for awhile," she said.

Neither "Jingles" nor Maxine let any grass grow under their feet, although Ingvar did plant a lawn, as we'll read later in *The Star*. In addition to raising three children, both seemed determined to fill out every minute of everyday.

Ingvar recalled, "After work at Valsetz I'd run my trap-line."

"At night?" I asked in amazement, knowing the rigorous demands of trapping—even in the daytime.

"Oh, sure," "Jingles replied. "I'd use a flashlight. Also, I had a dog trained to run ahead and find out if I'd caught anything in each trap."

Momentarily forgetting the Lamberts seemingly did everything together, Maxine added, "That's where we were on Pearl Harbor Day when the Japanese attacked. We were running our trapline. We hadn't heard about the attack on December 7th until we got home that evening."

"You took your new bride of six months trapping?" I questioned "Jingles."

"She loved it," he said with a mischievous grin, casting a sideways glance at his wife.

"We had a lot of fun together in the woods," Maxine confirmed.

The Valsetz Star weather report for July, 1941: "Warm sunshine every day for weeks. Kinda hot."

"Special Editor's Note: We have been reading a little about National Unity, but we wish all the nations could be friendly with each other. We wonder about all the boys and girls over on Hitler's land in Germany—would they play with us, we wonder—we are swimming and playing ping pong now.

Would they come over in our yard and take pictures and play with "Buck," Franklin's pup? Would they laugh with us or would they look at us and hate us?

We think maybe they would like us. And we know we would like them and when we were playing with them we wouldn't even think of

Hitler.

We would like to meet some Russian boys and girls and wouldn't it be funny if they liked us, and if we could hop over to Japan and maybe some Japanese boys and girls would grin at us.

We hope the world will shake hands and hurry up and get friendly again. We are very fond of friendly people."

"We are pleased to announce that we have been awarded an honorary membership in the *Oregon Newspaper Publishers* Association."

"Over in Russia there is a lot of terrible battle raging but we do not think Hitler will win. Stalin knows a lot of mean ways to do things too. They are both cruel and selfish and so they will fight and fight until they are both tired and that will give us more time to work and plan how we can help ourselves and England and maybe some of the other poor little countries."

"It seems the time will never come, when we can sit and sing,
  And loll around so lazy-like, not do a single thing.
  P.S. We have to practice piano 3-hours a day."

"Mr. Templeton, our publisher, says his reputation has suffered something fierce since we mentioned his name with Mae West's. If it gets any worse he says he will sue *The Valsetz Star* for damages.

We hope nobody says any more because we already owe him some money."

"It just seems like this month isn't very exciting. There is no queen, there are no princesses, no beautiful flowers, no airplane trips to Hollywood, no movie stars to see, no more ice cream with frozen roses on top.

Last night we had beans and cabbage for supper. This morning we had prunes."

"Jingles is back from his honeymoon and is piling lumber fast as lightning. Maxine is putting up ruffled curtains."

"Daddy will soon leave home on account of the, '*Hut Sut*' song.

"Mrs. Roosevelt said not to gossip about our neighbors. We haven't talked about anybody for two days."

"Stalin and Hitler fell out and the Valsetz baseball club got eliminated."

"Five babies were born and the logger's bath house burned down."

"Mr. Harris Ellsworth of the '*Roseburg News Review,*' Roseburg, Oregon, says production costs are going up and he doesn't think it is wise for us to expand at this time, like the pictures on page two of our deluxe edition, but we won't worry because Mr. Templeton, our publisher, hasn't sent us any extra bill yet."

"The Republicans are very calm and dignified. We are getting lonesome for them again."

"We got new sun suits and bought two new defense stamps."

"It's July and quite hot. We have been reading about the Republicans. Mr. Neil Allen has been named leader of the Republican State Central Committee to take Major Kern Crandall's place. Mr. Crandall is one of our subscribers and came to Valsetz with Mr. Starr, our Vice-President. We think Mr. Allen will be one of our subscribers soon."

"ADV. If you are hot and tired, and care no more to roam, buy some Cobbs & Mitchell lumber, build a house and stay at home."

WEDDING ANNIVERSARY
SUMMER–AUGUST, 1941

"How did you celebrate your fiftieth wedding anniversary in 1991?" I asked the youngish, Lambert seniors?

"I wanted to go to the Oregon Caves," Maxine replied. Instead, Jing took me white-water rafting. He said it would be more of an adventure than just climbing into a hole in the ground. We had a good time," she said. "Maybe we'll go to the caves for our sixtieth anniversary. It will soon be here."

The Lamberts have raised three children; Carl, who lives in Rainier, Washington; Linda, who retired from the navy and thirty years of government service; and Laura who is employed in the Eugene, Oregon school system.

"Carl resembles his dad," Maxine said. "It embarrasses him when I introduce him as, "my baby."

Maxine wanted her kids to grow up with an appreciation for good music. "Naturally, there were no music teachers in Valsetz, so I did the next best thing," she said. "I contacted a music teacher in town and paid him to ride 'The Skunk," (Railroad passenger car,) travel to Valsetz and give the kids music lessons." She also said that she and "Jingles" became involved in 4-H and Boy Scouts while the youngsters were growing up. "What an address we had," Maxine smiled, "a very comfy four-bedroom house right on the corner of Cadillac Avenue and Mud Alley."

Ingvar is quick to display his bank savings account book from the Falls City Bank, showing a balance of $4.60. "That was in 1929 and I lost my entire savings when the bank folded during the Depression," he said with a grin. "Not much by today's standards, but $4.60 was quite a bit of money in 1929."

Lambert remembers the "good old days," when he did his trading at Mack's General Store. "There were a lot more people living in

No trespassing allowed, a-foot, a-car, or on horseback. The former Valsetz townsite is behind this Boise-Cascade Co. sign. (Author photo)

town back in those days," he recalled. "I'm a Past Master of the Falls City Masonic Lodge, too," he said.

In 1955, "Jingles" became a T-V star when Arlene Frances came to Portland with her entourage. She filmed him at the Portland Forestry Center which was billed as the largest log cabin in the world before it burned in August, 1964. Although he couldn't get much height inside the building, Ingvar put on a "low-level," high-climbing exhibition. Hugh Downs, and prolific Northwest author, Stewart Holbrook, were included in the group. Arlene Frances gave Lambert an autographed picture of herself, "To my favorite high-climber."

*　*　*　*　*　*

The August, 1941 weather forecast in *The Star* went like this: "Foggy mornings and cool days."

"Special Editor's Note: We haven't thought very much about the war and we don't see why people in Europe have to fight and grab and kill when it's so nice and cool down at the swimming hole.

We are still planning on having all of our eight-hundred subscribers to a great big party and we will have ice cream and if there isn't enough ice cream we will have green apples. We would have Mrs. Roosevelt and Adeline Merriam Conner and Wendell Willkie and Carrie Jacobs Bond and Black Jim of Fort Wayne, Indiana who is one of our best subscribers, and Mrs. Roosevelt wouldn't mind if he sat beside her, and Katie who is the largest woman in Roaring Gulch, Pennsylvania and is a strong Republican could sit by Wendell Willkie. But John Davey who lives on Lake Michigan would have to sit by himself because he gets so terribly mad when we say something nice about the Democrats. We would have games and our subscribers could chat and visit all day and then stay for supper."

"If Secretary of State Earl Snell runs for Governor of Oregon against Governor Sprague, we won't know what to do. They are both Republicans, and both very friendly to us. We have received several letters from Governor Sprague and once at Senator McNary's nomination luncheon at Fir Cone, we had our picture taken with him, but every Christmas for four years we have received a letter from Secretary of State Earl Snell saying how much he enjoyed *The Star*, and then in April this year he came to Valsetz and shook hands with everybody and smiled at Mother, and now we don't know what to do."

"We have been going all over Valsetz to get aluminum for the National Aluminum Drive. But nobody has much. We got a few old pie tins, and an egg poacher.

Daddy threw in his brand new aluminum cocktail shaker because he said he would do anything to beat Hitler.

One woman said she would give her son but she needed her pots and pans."

"Marshall Petain went over on Germany's side. At school we

186

would die before we would go over on the other side."

"President Roosevelt and Prime Minister Churchill met in the middle of the ocean for a short visit and the Bridge Club met over at the Thomas house. It will make history."

"ADV. Jingles now has settled down, and going to build a house.
He looked for lumber every place, so he could please his spouse.
He looked around for days and days, and fell for every fad.
When Maxine saw the mess he'd made, oh boy! did she get mad.
Now Jingles, love, just listen here, and calm yourself my dear,
Why look around and shop for grief when Cobbs & Mitchell's near.
Just use the phone and hurry now, and tell your neighbors too
That Cobbs & Mitchell's lumber is so nice and smooth and new!"

"Valsetz has had several tragedies this month. One man almost lost his head, one man broke his hip, and one man killed his cousin because he thought he was a deer."

"John Ryan left Valsetz after working hard for nine years."

"Mrs. Fee, our fortune teller, has left Valsetz but none of the fortunes ever came true anyway."

"Mother doesn't care if the silk stockings are all gone. She said they were always full of runs anyway."

"Mrs. Heydon, our post mistress, is learning the rhumba."

"Mrs. Thomas got tired of her family and went to Portland and stayed two weeks."

"Valsetz hasn't had any fires this year. We hope all our loggers will knock on wood,"

"One of our loggers got hurt and one got married."

"We are learning to bake bread, but Mother gave the only pan she had to mix anything in to the Government."

"Franklin, not Franklin Roosevelt, but Franklin the Asssistant Editor of the *Star* is freezing all his cash. He won't even buy an ice cream cone."

"Mrs. Babb, Grandma Babb, and all the little Babbs went to Bandon to get away from it all."

"We have the fastest loggers in Oregon. At the annual String Bean Festival at Stayton, Oregon (Daddy was born there), Al Poole, one of our loggers, sawed a 32-inch log right through the middle in three minutes and three seconds. He has bushy hair and a gay smile and five children. He got twenty-five dollars and a real sharp saw."

THE HOBBY ROOM
SUMMER–SEPTEMBER, 1941

Reminscing about his fur trapping days, "Jingles" got that far away look in his bright and sparkly eyes as he recounted, "Mostly we trapped mink and muskrat. Occasionally I'd catch a bobcat and that was worth $100.00 because there was a state bounty on bobcats and cougars. Boy, that was big money in those days. I guess the state wanted to cut down on the cat population because they killed so many game birds and small animals."

Ingvar's facial expression would change to that of a mischevious young man when he said, "Well, on occasion a beaver might mistakenly wander into one of our traps, it just couldn't be helped," he said in a semi-innocent tone. For many years beaver were a protected species, but their fur was valuable.

The Lambert spare bedroom became Maxine and "Jing's" hobby room. "I peeled cascara bark in my spare time and they paid more when it was dried so I spread it out in the bedroom to dry," he said. "In Valsetz you'd need a month of Sundays to dry anything outside."

Lambert continued, "During trapping season I stretched my pelts on boards and dried them in the spare room. The mill superintendent stopped by for a visit with us once and he asked about the unusual smell in the house. I hated to tell him it was caused by my trapping and bark peeling."

"This guy always has to be doing something," Maxine said about her husband. I remember one year in Valsetz when he turned my kitchen into a ski factory."

That comment brought a hearty laugh from Ingvar. "Oh yes, I remember," he said. "I had to boil water on the kitchen stove so I could put the right bend in the wood. The wax had to be heated and I warmed the skis with her flat irons before applying the wax."

Following Pearl Harbor, and the beginning of WWII, Ingvar Lambert tried to enlist and fight for his adopted country in its time of need. "I tried to get into the service several times, but the local selective service board always came up with an excuse why they wouldn't take me," he recalled. "I think my employer, Cobbs & Mitchell had a reason for me staying on the job. Once I even quit them, but they still wouldn't take me. Let me tell you, it made me doggone mad."

*   *   *   *   *   *

It was a dreary weather forecast for September, 1941 in *The Star*:

"Buckets of rain to come down yet, not much chance for any change."

"Special Editor's Note: We have been saying our prayers for a long time, and always we have prayed for peace, but now it doesn't seem to do any good.

We listened to President Roosevelt's last speech over the radio, and he says if he sees a rattlesnake with its head reared up, he will pop it one and there won't be any time to pray. He won't stand for any more smarty business.

Franklin, not Franklin Roosevelt the President, but Franklin Thomas, the Assistant Editor of *The Star*, says he is glad now that he took so many vitamins only he wishes he hadn't gotten his gun so many Christmases back on account of it being kind of rusty now. He thinks Patrick Henry was swell and he thinks his, 'Give Me Liberty or Give Me Death,' was the best thing anybody ever said except President Roosevelt shook his fist through the radio and said, 'Don't come another step closer!'

Well, we are standing behind our President and Franklin said he thought he could get the rust off his gun with some oil and this winter we will take some knitting lessons.

We are sorry the prayers didn't work."

"We received a letter from Secretary of State Earl Snell and he is terribly grieved if he has caused us any confusion, and he said if he could only receive the support of *The Valsetz Star* he would come to Valsetz on a moment's notice and shake hands again and again, but he didn't say anything about smiling at Mother again!

And Lew Wallace is also running for something but Daddy said we didn't have to worry about him because he is a Democrat and would probably be elected anyway."

"Mr. Templeton, our publisher, has gained ten pounds this year and his BVD's won't button in front. It's on account of the lumber business being so good."

"We have just received notice from 'Avon House,' New York, that one of our citizens of Valsetz, Mr. George King who writes poetry and works in the mill, has won a place in the 'Book of Modern Poetry, the American First Edition' an eight-hundred page volume just published."

"Mr. Howard B. Hall of Portland wants to know whether or not we are acquainted with Mr. Herbert Templeton, of Portland. We nearly died; he is our publisher and best friend."

"We can't have the big party in our back yard because Reller's cow has been there."

"Mr. Seneca Fouts, Portland attorney, said, 'The Valsetz Star gives to a tired and clouded world gleams of sunshine, lightness and joy."

"Once we were mad at President Roosevelt and all the Democrats but we don't talk about that. We will talk about it again as soon as the war is over though."

"We sent a dollar to London, England to help lick Hitler. We are tired of him taking everything."

"ADV. Now that fall is coming, and you're getting something new, order Cobbs & Mitchell's lumber, it's the smartest thing to do."

"Jingles is sitting on his front porch gazing at his green lawn. Maxine came out with a plate of hot ginger cookies. He is glad he got married."

"Mrs. Fraser, our best bridge player, has a cold in her nose. She knows where every ace is."

"One of our loggers had his shoes slung over his shoulder and went tramping down the highway singing. He was glad to be alive."

"Franklin's dog, 'Buck,' died and Leonard had a baby."

"Mrs. Haydon got discouraged with the rhumba."

"Miss Jane Templeton, our publisher's pretty daughter of United Airlines, will be married to a great big Spokane insurance man in October. She graduated from Scripps and University of Washington. He picks her up and carries her."

"Paul Lowe left to join the U.S. Army and get twenty-one dollars a month and a new suit."

"Donald Denno is working in the planing mill so he can go back to the University of Oregon next year."

"Mrs. Frank Wilson of Klamath Falls wrote and said, 'God bless and keep you and yours 'neath the shelter of His everlasting arms.' We feel much better."

"FLASH: We have just discovered how we can have the big party for all our subscribers. Read all the details in the October issue of *The Star*."

FALLS CITY
AUTUMN–OCTOBER, 1941

The closest center of retail stores for Valsetz had always been in Falls City, a rigorous 16-mile drive over a twisty, sometimes gravelled, never paved road. Prior to construction of the Valsetz road, the only way in and out of the lumber community was via the Valley and Siletz Railroad into Hoskins and Independence where connections could be made onto the Southern Pacific.

Falls City acquired its name from the picturesque falls on the Little Luckiamute river which actually divides the town.

The name was a compromise with promoters who wanted to call the place Luckiamute Falls in the 1890's.

Outdoor activities and the beauty of the falls originally attracted visitors to the area. Developers had planned a grandiose resort for hunters, fisherpeople and campers on a knob north of town but it never materialized. The first commercial enterprise was a grist mill built near the falls, in 1852, by John Thorp and subsequently moved to Rickreall, (then Dixie) about twelve years later.

The few locals received their mail at a post office in Syracuse, located about a mile east. In 1891 the post office was moved to Falls City, with A.M. Bryant as postmaster. Mail arrived twice a week.

Try as they might not to become just another Oregon sawmill town, the tall timber of the area attracted lumbermen like bears to a honey-tree. The first sawmill was erected near the town by John Montgomery. Diversification through agriculture temporarily competed with lumber as the primary cash crop, but wood was always dominant. A large sawmill built in 1901 by Bryan and Lucas was sold to Cobbs & Mitchell, our Valsetz founders. In the early 1900's, nearly twenty large and small sawmills were spittin' sawdust in the immediate area.

During the early 1900's the population of the burgh grew to nearly

1,000. But when Cobbs & Mitchell moved their operations in 1922 to the new mill in Valsetz, they took a good chunk of the Falls City populace with them.

Today, the sleepy little town provides a pleasant shruburban living area on the Valsetz "road to nowhere." The "Little Lucky" still tumbles down the falls, a few log truck loads of woodpecker poles pass through, and local residents enjoy their laid back lifestyle in their isolated little corner of Polk County, Oregon.

*   *   *   *   *   *

The Valsetz weather forecast for October: "Rain will fall all the time now."

"Special Editor's Note: At last we have completed all arrangements for the big party for our subscribers.

So many of our subscribers back in New York and the East couldn't come so far away as Valsetz for just one afternoon, and besides people were very fussy whom they sat beside. Adeline Merriam Conner wanted to sit by Mrs. Roosevelt to feel of her stockings and see if they were really cotton like she said. Everybody wanted to sit by Mrs. Roosevelt except Robert Tedlow of Detroit, Michigan who wanted to sit by Joe Louis, but Joe isn't one of our subscribers. One man said, 'Don't put me beside a Democrat.'

And so now we have set the important date which is on November 5th at 7 p.m., Pacific Standard Time, which will be 8 p.m. Mountain Standard Time, 9 p.m. Central Standard Time and 10 p.m. Eastern Standard Time, and for our one subscriber in Nova Scotia it will be 11 p.m. In Europe it will be the next morning, but everybody is busy fighting over there so we won't bother them.

So will each and every one of our subscribers please sit down at exactly the above time on November 5th and eat a dish of ice cream and think of each other and the editor and the assistant editor and Mr. Templeton, our publisher. Hundreds of our subscribers will be doing exactly the same thing at the same time.

And while thinking of each other and eating ice cream, will everyone please bow their heads a moment for a quick little prayer that somebody will soon get Hitler.

We would like to receive some letters from our subscribers so we will know if they enjoyed the 'party.'

If there is anybody who doesn't care to pray will they please bow their head and think of Mr. Templeton, our publisher.

People don't have to be subscribers to bow their heads at 7 p.m. on November 5th."

"They are saving paper over in England. Mr. Christiansen's letter was typewritten on a tiny narrow piece of paper. We are wasting paper in America."

"ADV. Mr. Chas G. Briggs, President of 'The Booth-Kelly Lumber Co.' of Eugene, sent us the following ad to put in the October *Star*:
'If Cobbs & Mitchell lumber does not quite fill the bill,
 You might try our Booth-Kelly whose stock is better still.'"

"Answer: Now Booth-Kelly lumber might be free of every knot,
But compared to COBBS & MITCHELL it isn't very hot.
It probably is an awful price, we warn you, don't get caught!
Order quick from COBBS & MITCHELL when you plan a house and lot."

"Frances Keller of Buffalo, New York said she has never seen the West but has learned to love it through *The Star*. She is an artist and some time will 'travel out west' and see our hemlock and fir trees and the blue Pacific and the Valsetz rain and Jingles and Maxine. She said,

'They sound so cozy and would make anybody want to get married.'"

"Crowds of people went from Valsetz to see the Oregon State-Stanford Victory game. The victory was for Oregon State."

"Miss Mary Leslie Chandler of 10 Downing Street, New York City—not London—said in her letter, 'All the evening I have been longing for some hot ginger cookies, the thick soft kind like grandmother used to make. Lucky Jingles!'"

"And a girl named Lois who lives in Chicago but we can't give her last name or street number, wants to marry a Valsetz logger. We will write and let her know."

"A young lady in New York City said she wished she could have married Jingles. She believes he would have been just the type for her. She said there wasn't a man in New York City who would protect a woman. She sounded terribly mad."

"Next month we are announcing our choice of candidate for Governor of Oregon. We are coming out for somebody. We are taking a stand. We will put up posters and pass out cards. We will do anything to get our candidate elected. It will be fun. It will be a Republican, too."

"We have been invited to become a member of '*The State Woman's Press Club.*'"

INDEPENDENCE
AUTUMN–NOVEMBER, 1941

Named for the famous Missouri jumping off place of many western-bound wagon trains in the mid-1800's, Independence, Oregon, became the final destination for a passel of early pioneers. The town's originator was E.A. Thorp, son of Falls City grist mill entrepreneur, John Thorp. Good-hearted E.A. had given Thomas Burbank two lots he had platted in Independence, with the stipulation the Burbanks would build there, and Thorp would name the place after his hometown in Missouri.

The town really got off the ground in 1885 when the Governor and legislative assembly approved a charter for the city of Independence. Leonard Williams became the first postmaster when the Independence post office had first opened in the rear of a log cabin general store in 1853.

Two competing townsites merged in the late 1860's, forming one town of Independence. Businesses identified in 1867 included a hotel, spirits purveyor, grain and produce dealer, blacksmith, general merchandise store, stockman and post office. In 1879, a fire department bucket brigade was formed and a hand fire engine was bought in 1883. A disastrous Willamette river flood swept a portion of the town downriver in 1890.

Train service arrived in Independence in 1886 with the coming of the Oregon-Western railroad. Telephones came on line in 1885 and an opera house opened in 1888. At about the same time, several steamships plied the river providing passenger and freight service, Corvallis to Portland.

Independence saw its first automobile in 1907 when a prominent doctor bought a Reo Horseless buggy. The town council strictly enforced a speed limit of six-miles per hour.

During the early 1900's, the town became known as the "Hop

Center of the World." During hop picking season the Independence population would balloon to more than 10,000 people with the tremendous influx of pickers. The Independence-Monmouth Railroad was 2.5 miles long and became well-known as the shortest railroad in the world, later incorporated into the Southern Pacific. Millions of board-feet of Valsetz lumber was shipped by rail through Independence.

At one time, many celebrated Oregon personalities called the town on the Willamette home, including U.S. Senator Charles McNary and former Oregon Governor, Isaac Patterson.

* * * * * *

In Valsetz, Dorothy Anne and Franklin were celebrating the fourth anniversary of *The Valsetz Star*:

"Just four years ago Mr. Templeton published our first copy. We were terribly strong Republicans then and we just couldn't bear Democrats. But we were only nine years old then and didn't know much. Now we are old and have met some awfully nice Democrats who have taken a great interest in our paper, and so we have become quite broad and are standing behind our President Roosevelt fierce and strong.

WE WILL WIN THE WAR! We—Franklin Thomas and the editor—defy all of Europe to come and get us. THEY CAN'T DO IT! We are giving up everything and saving on paper and using the stubs of left-over pencils and buying government savings stamps instead of 'Coca-Colas.' We are suffering but we are glad."

"We think our ice cream party was a great success.
We have received many letters and on the eve of the party we got a whole stack of telegrams.

Everybody gathered in little groups, ate ice cream and bowed their heads.

One subscriber said he didn't like ice cream so he took a little nip of 'Old Crow,' but he bowed his head just the same.

Another subscriber in Billings, Montana, said it was the first party he ever attended where he had to buy his own ice cream.

Mr. Ronald Belknap of Rochester, New York said he bought some ice cream, took it over to his girl's house and proposed to her. She accepted and they bowed their heads together and will be married on Christmas Day. He said 'Hooray for *The Star.*'

A few accidents occurred. When Frank J. Bowers of Traverse City, Michigan, bowed his head he couldn't think of anybody but Hitler and he got so mad he burned himself."

"In spite of the words at the top of this column, this is still a very strong Republican paper."

"A great many of our subscribers have wanted to know how Valsetz got such a queer name. We asked Mrs. Heydon, our postmistress, who came over the hill on horseback thirty years ago and has been here ever since, and she told us that away back in 1914 when they started to build a railroad from Independence into the Siletz Basin to tap the timber holdings of Cobbs & Mitchell, they named the railroad Valley & Siletz, because it crossed the Willamette Valley and ran into the Siletz Basin. Then later when they decided to build a town and name it, they thought it fitting to honor the railroad that opened this vast timber tract.

"Mr. Walter Inch who was Cobbs & Mitchell's civil engineer at the time, thought Valley & Siletz was too long a name for the future generations to write. And so one day while he was standing at the crossroads and pondering on shortening the name, a black bear came out of the bushes and Mr. Inch just yelled, 'Valsetz,' and ran for his life.

The Indians were afraid of the Siletz basin after Cobbs & Mitchell built their new town, but the engineers soon convinced them that aside from wildcats, bears, cougars, deer, beaver, blackberries and Mrs. Heydon, there was nothing to fear."

"We've decided not to come out for anybody in the governor's election as Daddy said he might want to run for Congress some day and besides if we should meet one or the other on the street in Salem, one or the other might not speak to us."

"We don't know what to do about priorities."

"ADV. When we talk of Cobbs & Mitchell,
    People say we have a line,
    But you know we really mean it,
    When we say their lumber's fine."

"Mrs. Emory, Mrs. Shurman, and Mrs. Bagley, all ladies past fifty and all members of the Lavender Club of Portland, came to Valsetz to visit the Grouts. Mrs. Emory came to get a logger but Mrs. Shurman and Mrs. Bagley didn't want one."

"Your editor is attending Parrish Junior High School in Salem this year. We have a Pep Club and yell our heads off. It's a swell school."

"Mr. George H. Riches, a banker of Salem, said he bet that Hitler's ears were pretty red on the night of the ice cream party."

"And now we wish to make an announcement and it's quite hard to make, but next month, with the December issue—we are suspending publication of *The Valsetz Star.*

The old and the new above former Valsetz. A rotted stump, possibly logged during the Valsetz heyday, stands a lonely vigil over a plateau of more recently logged stumps. Fanno Ridge in the distance hosts a new crop, probably third-growth, of dark green Douglas firs. (Author photo)

We are folding up our card table and closing our door. We are going out of business.

If we owe anybody any money, we hope they won't get excited. We hope they will be calm and we will pay them as soon as we get all of our business settled.

We are going to be very lonely without all the nice letters from our friends and subscribers.

And now good-bye until next month, when we will tell you more about it."

"Weather forecast: It will just keep pouring down until after Christmas."

THE LAST HURRAH!
AUTUMN–DECEMBER 1941

Like a bolt out of the blue, Dorothy Anne shocked her readers with this announcement:

"When our readers receive this, our last and farewell edition of *The Valsetz Star*, people will be hurrying about buying Christmas gifts and all the world will seem happy, but there are some who will be unhappy and lonely, so we will try to cheer them with an exta copy or two of our Christmas number.

All the time we've published *The Star*, we've enjoyed sending out a great many free copies to ones who couldn't afford to subscribe. We would like our regular subscribers to know we've enjoyed getting the money, too!

For three years we have been sending *The Star* to an Old Folks' Home in Philadelphia where a great number of people stay. We send several copies and when they arrive all the old ladies and gentlemen gather in the living room and someone reads the paper aloud, and one really old lady wrote, 'Thanks, my dear, for bringing a great deal of joy into our lives.'

Last night we had a letter from a man who has been receiving *The Star* for the past two years. He is a prisoner in Michigan State Penitentiary and had just received word that he was being released from prison. He will be free again. He is a mechanic and will get a job and help with the defense work. He wrote right away to thank us and tell us how much he and his fellow prisoners had laughed over each copy of *The Star*.

Thank you, our dear prison friend. We don't think you are very bad.

Then the two hospitals where *The Star* is read by all the patients right straight through the building and did we ever tell our later subscribers that once Mrs. Roosevelt threw her head back and laughed while reading *The Star* at her weekly press club. She thought it was funny about the Republicans and the Democrats.

But everything hasn't always been funny, though. One of our subscribers in Montana owned a very fine and valuable horse. One night while he was reading his copy of *The Star* (the man, not the horse) out in the barn it suddenly blew into the stall and the horse ate it and died the next day. But our subscriber wrote and said he was pretty sure it was the mildewed oats."

"We are going on the air for a grand farewell party. We will broadcast direct from Valsetz high in the Coast Range mountains on Saturday, December 13th, from five until five-thirty over KOIN and the 'Columbia Broadcasting System,' all stations from Chicago, west. Mr. Swartwood, program manager for KOIN, says there will be a mike right in *The Star* office, another one close to the big head saw in the mill, and two or three others around Valsetz.

You will hear Jingles on how to have a green lawn, and Maxine with her best recipe for hot ginger cookies.

You will hear Mrs. Heydon tell how she fought wild animals in the early days. And Donald Denno who addresses our envelopes and is working his way through the planing mill and the University of Oregon, will tell you how he almost gives up at times.

There will be a word from Mother and Daddy, and Mr. Templeton, our publisher, and Franklin's papa, who is superintendent of Cobbs and Mitchell.

So tune in Saturday night, December 13th, from five to five-thirty over CBS."

"A great many of our readers are shocked because we are giving up *The Star*.

One man said if we needed any money he would send us plenty.

The main street of Falls city, Oregon as it appears today. (Author photo)

But no, it isn't that. We are kind of shocked too but your editor is away at school this year in Salem and there are music and vocal lessons and no time left for anything except the Parrish Pep Club."

"We have a great many people to thank for the success of *The Star*.

We wish especially to thank the Oregon newspapers who have regularly written articles on our paper over a period of four years. They have given us valuable space on their front pages and editorial sections. We thank them here and now, and wish them a very Merry Christmas.

And in the east, the '*Baltimore Sun,*' the '*New York Herald-Tribune,*' the '*Philadelphia Inquirer,*' the '*Christian Science Monitor,*' the '*Denver Post,*' the "*New York Sun,*' the '*Los Angeles Herald,*' the '*Oakland Tribune,*' and the '*Washington, D.C. Post.*' And many other newspapers throughout the United State who have given space to *The Star*. Each and every one we wish to thank.

And the radio stations and Art Kirkham and our publisher, Mr.

Herbert Templeton, of whom we once said when we were only nine years old, "We think he is a very kind man." Now we are thirteen and we know he is a kind man.

He has given us much of his time and we've used thousands of sheets of his paper. It's a good thing we are going out of business because paper is getting high."

"Thank you, everybody, each and every one—for cheering letters—we've kept every one and have a trunk full—for your encouraging words—for suggestions—for subscriptions—we've kept every one." (Note: On one record day during the life of *The Valsetz Star*, Dorothy Anne received 42 letters just from the New York area alone.)

PASSING IN REVIEW

"And now the grand finale, as you all pass in review,
We'll take a little time out, with a word for you, and you.
First we see our Jingles coming, pacing down the strand,
He's stepping high and fearless, holding Maxine by the hand.
And next is Mrs. Heydon, who's been here so many years,
She's grappled long with man and beast, 'til not a thing she fears.
And here comes Cobbs & Mitchell, with their lumber nice and smooth,
They'll surely do you lots of good, when your nerves you try to soothe.
Over there is Mrs. Roosevelt, we've often used her name,
But what cares she, a woman who's been always used to fame.
And here we see our publisher, he's leading up the rear,
He shot *The Star* across the land, his friends are far and near.
And now please meet my Mother, who's had lots of trouble too,
 With gas upon her stomach, and corsets old and new.
That's Daddy standing quite close by, and says, 'What's this about?'
And though he talks an awful lot, it's hard to leave him out.

You see that column passing there? Our subscribers fierce and strong,
Just place your bet on any one, and boy you won't go wrong.
And now *The Star* is fading, and goodbyes are being said,
But always we'll remember you, in the happy years ahead."

"We've had lots of fun in the last four years, and we hope we haven't hurt anybody's feelings.

We are sad about saying goodbye, Mother is sitting in the living room, rocking and crying.

Goodbye again, have a Merry Christmas.

And now we are all crying."

The welcome sign to Falls City, Oregon. The little town is located in the Little Luckiamute River valley, home of the "Mighty Mountaineers," and the October mushroom festival. (Author photo)

Epilogue

As Dorothy Anne Hobson closed her playhouse door on the *Valsetz Star's* office, shutting down publication, she also closed the door on her writing career. "I had told the *Portland City Club* that I would not pursue a journalistic profession," she said. Dorothy's decision to retire her stubby writing pencil was received with dismay by many Northwest, and national newspaper people. "Truly a wasted talent", groused one editor.

The bright-eyed former editor completed Parrish Junior High in Salem, then attended high school at Portland's St. Helens Hall. She enrolled at Salem's Willamette University in 1946, majoring in Political Science. It was in the Capitol City's prestigious University that she met Frederick H. Graham. They were married on August 20, 1949. Dorothy acquiesced to her husband's career as a teacher, principal and superintendent of education, seemingly content to wear the apron strings and raise their three children.

In the early 1960's, Dorothy and Frederick jointly operated the Santiam Hardware Store. Later, she dabbled in real estate and interior decorating.

In August, 1970, Dorothy suffered a debilitating stroke, causing partial paralysis, initially confining her to a wheelchair. Determined to overcome her immobility, Dorothy willed her indomitable spirit to make her strong and subsequently, got back on her feet.

Frederick Graham passed away in Colton, Oregon, in 1980, having become a "gentleman farmer," for the last few years of his life. Ruby Hobson, Dorothy's mother, and guiding light during the days of the *Valsetz Star*, died in 1978. Dorothy's father, Henry Hobson, died in 1987.

Fittingly, Dorothy was honored as an invited guest at the last graduating class from Valsetz High school on May 26, 1984, just prior to the razing of the town by "*Boise-Cascade*." Nine seniors received diplomas in the school's gymnasium. Dorothy and an audience estimated at 300, heard guest speaker, U.S. Senator, Mark O. Hatfield (R-OR) as he emphasized that humankind was resilient, always adapting to unfortunate setbacks.

Dorothy suffered a fall in 1992, complicating her condition from the earlier stroke and causing her to be house-bound most of the time. With her death, in 1996, Oregon and the nation could remember Dorothy Anne as the whimsical young editor whose pragmatic and satirical writings brought the backwoods logging community of Valsetz, Oregon, to national attention.

At one time, she was quoted as proclaiming, "My name is Dorothy Anne Hobson Graham and there is nobody like me in the entire world."

And you know what? She was probably right.

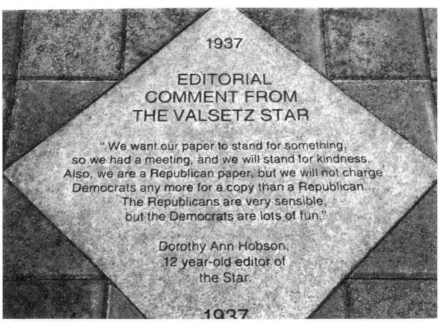

Sidewalk plaques capture the history of well-known Oregonians in walkways around the state capitol building and grounds. This stone epitaph commemorates Dorothy Anne Hobson and her Valsetz Star. She was nine-years old in 1937, not twelve. (Photo courtesy Graham family)